for my mum and dad and craig, without whom this book would never have happened

Art direction and design Vanessa Courtier · **Food styling** Angela Boggiano · **Publishing manager** Anna Cheifetz

Angela's Assistant Jules Mercer · **Recipe still-life photography** Craig Robertson · **Location and reportage photography** Vanessa Courtier

For the 2013 edition **Commissioning Editor** Eleanor Maxfield · **Senior Art Editor** Juliette Norsworthy · **Project Editor** Joanne Wilson
Production Controller Sarah Kramer

An Hachette UK Company
www.hachette.co.uk

First published in Great Britain in 2006 by Cassell Illustrated

This edition published 2013 by Mitchell Beazley, a division of Octopus Publishing Group Limited,
189 Shaftesbury Avenue, London WC2H 8JY

Distributed in the US by Hachette Book Group USA, 237 Park Avenue, New York, NY 10017, USA
Distributed in Canada by Canadian Manda Group, 165 Dufferin Street, Toronto, Ontario, Canada M6K 3H6
www.octopusbooksusa.com

Text copyright © Angela Boggiano 2006, 2013   Design and layout © Octopus Publishing Group Limited 2013

The moral right of Angela Boggiano to be identified as the author of this Work has been asserted
in accordance with the Copyright, Designs and Patents Act of 1988

A CIP catalogue record for this book is available from the British Library.

ISBN-13: 978-1-84533-766-7

Printed in China

pie

Angela Boggiano

photography by Vanessa Courtier and Craig Robertson

MITCHELL BEAZLEY

contents

"I've always loved pies. Making them, eating them, watching how other people make them, talking about them. In fact, talking about them was probably what inspired me to write this book more than anything else. I began to realize what an emotional issue pies are for many people. Almost everyone has a favorite pie, and with that pie comes a story, often about a family member or childhood memory. Favorite pies are not necessarily gourmet pies—usually a humble apple pie that Auntie Maureen used to make or a pork pie from the local butchers. It's often the nostalgia and comforting thoughts they conjure up that make the pies seem to taste all the more delicious.

As I carried out more and more research, I realized just how large a part pie making plays in this country's heritage. Britain is steeped in pie-making traditions, from Cornish pasties to game pies. It's easy to see why pies are so popular; a pie is a warming, filling complete meal in itself—eaten in the hand for lunches and picnics as well as a hearty main meal. Actually, I think the pie is the greatest invention ever, but maybe that makes me a bit of a pie obsessive!

As well as tasty recipes, I wanted to include stories of pie makers old and new from the wonderful heritage of the famous British pie and mash shops to the modern pie café with its contemporary fillings. That's why this book contains a collection of traditional recipes, such as stargazy pie and raised pies with hot-water crust pastry, alongside more modern pies with tasty fillings, like lamb, mint and pumpkin, or curried soccer pie.

Pies don't need fancy fillings with hundreds of ingredients—they can be relatively simple—but the ingredients do need to be of high quality to make a pie really stand out. If you always choose good meat you won't need to do much to the filling apart from cooking it slowly to capture its delicious flavor. Tasty local and regional cheeses, seasonal fruits and vegetables can only add to a successful end result.

Making a spectacular pie will give you a real sense of achievement. Perhaps it's because pie making does take a bit of time and effort that the sense of satisfaction is so great. But—and this is the big but—despite the effort, pie making is not something to be scared of, and I hope that's what you'll find with this collection of recipes. I wanted to take away the fear of pastry making—which is what stops most people making pies—because the fillings are generally straightforward. I want everybody to make pies and to create a new generation of pie makers so that all the fascinating history surrounding them is not lost. Go forth and bake!

"

historypie

Since recipes have first been recorded, the pie has held an honored place in the history of cooking. Certainly the British have as great a claim as any nation to being the ultimate exponents of the art of pie making. From the earliest medieval recipes to substantial eighteenth-century pies, a tradition has grown up that is an integral part of our culinary heritage.

There is evidence, however, that the ancient Egyptians may have been the first to indulge, and that recipes were passed from Egypt to classical Greece and then to Rome and the rest of Europe. In the earliest recipes it is clear that the pastry was never eaten but used merely as a container to be thrown away and as a malleable material to make sculptural forms. Known as "subtleties," these forms became very popular in medieval England and were used as centerpieces for banqueting tables. The English were also responsible for creating pastry using suet and fat (later butter), in place of the oil used by the Romans. This allowed the evolution of finer and more delicate pastry, which ultimately could be eaten.

The great advantage of the pie has always been that it allows for a range of ingredients to be cooked together in a pastry crust, making it as popular in the banqueting hall as in the home. The only differentiation has been in the ingredients used. Traditionally the lowest form of pie was "umble pie," made from the entrails of deer and served to the less fortunate diners at the medieval dinner table (where the phrase "to eat humble pie" was coined). More esteemed diners might, however, be tucking into a delicious venison pie, or perhaps a pie of seasonal fruits.

Pies were versatile, portable, and easy to cook; and the discovery that pouring clarified butter into the pastry casing excluded any air and preserved the contents for a time only increased pies' popularity, as they could be stored and transported farther afield—the ultimate traveling fare.

With recipes taken to America and Australia by the first English settlers, the pie furthered its global domination. From savory to sweet, shortcrust (plain) to flaky, today's favorite pies are now the culmination of a long and varied heritage that continues to inform every exciting new filling and delicious pie creation.

basicpie

For me, the best bit of a pie is the golden crust, so the more there is of that the better. Making pastry isn't difficult if you follow a few simple rules and master the basic techniques—there's a lot of truth in the old saying "as easy as pie." Homemade crust always has a better flavor than store-bought and it's this taste and texture that make the process really worthwhile and quite satisfying. One of the benchmarks of cooking, however, is authenticity, and mastering the classic look of the "turned-out" pie-shop pie can become a labor of love. Producing a beautiful homemade pie involves a number of stages and it can't be simply bashed out. So, whether you opt for making your own or using store-bought, pastry dough will always require a little patience and respect.

Here are my golden rules for achieving perfect results when making your own pastry dough:

1 Handle it lightly
2 Keep it cool
3 Bake it in a hot oven

all you need for pastry

Hands   Cool hands are the cook's most valuable asset.

Flour   Plain white all-purpose flour is the most widely used flour for shortcrust pastry. Self-rising flour produces a much softer pastry, which can be a little difficult to handle, and gives a very crumbly texture when you want a crisp pastry crust.

Choose an all-purpose flour for flaky and puff pastry and a breadmaking flour for hot-water crust pastry (as for this you need plenty of gluten to shape the pastry). The best way to store flour is in its own bag (as this will have the use-by date on it) in a cool dry place. Try not to mix new flour with old stock.

Fat   The fat is such an important feature in pastry, as it determines the texture as well as the taste. Always weigh your fat carefully—too much fat will make the pastry unmanageable and very short (crumbly) and too little will make it hard. Lard is the vital ingredient in hot-water crust pastry.

A mixture of shortening and butter makes a very good shortcrust pastry as the shortening gives it a short, light and crisp texture and the butter imparts a delicious flavor. Don't be tempted to substitute margarine as it contains water and will result in a tough crust. Ensure that the fat is cool but not straight from the refrigerator as this makes it tricky to handle. Do not use low-fat butter.

Eggs   Egg yolks are added to pastry to enrich the dough, creating a rich shortcrust pastry. Eggs are also used for glazes, especially on savory pies. A mixture of equal quantities of egg yolk and water and a pinch of salt gives the best ever golden glaze.

Liquid   Water is the main liquid used in pastry making, but milk can also be added. Adding sour cream or yogurt will make a tender pastry, ideal for en croûtes and wrapping pâtés. Pastry with a high fat content and the addition of egg yolks needs hardly any water. In most cases the liquid should be chilled so that it does not soften or melt the fat. The exception is hot-water crust pastry where the fat and liquid must be hot. Be careful when adding the liquid—too much will make your dough sticky and difficult to handle and tough when cooked; too little and it will be dry and may crack.

Containers   For the best results when making a double-crust pie, use a metallic pie pan. I use enamel pans, which work well as they come in various sizes and are inexpensive. Ceramic dishes just don't conduct the heat well enough to get the bottom of the pie crisp.

Pie plates have a wide rim and are usually made of metal. They are quite shallow and can also be used to make a double-crust pie, which can then be cut into wedges for serving.

Deep earthenware pie dishes, which can be round or oval, are great for rich, robust, savory or sweet fillings that are quite chunky and require only one crust of pastry on the top.

Raised pie molds are ideal for raised game and meat pies. They are normally hinged on one side so that you can remove the pie easily when it is cooked. They also often have patterned sides which give the pie an embossed appearance when it is turned out.

Pie funnel   This ceramic funnel acts as a chimney as the pie filling cooks, letting out steam which might otherwise make the pastry soggy and prevent it from rising properly. The funnel also provides extra support for the pastry.

Baking sheet   A heavy-duty baking sheet is a real asset for crisping the pastry on the bottom of your pie. Place the baking sheet in a hot oven for about 15 minutes to heat up thoroughly, then sit the pie on the hot sheet and bake. The heat from the sheet will help to ensure a crispy bottom. The sheet will also catch any spillages from the pie if the filling bubbles out (which certainly saves on the oven cleaning!).

Rolling pin   A rolling pin is, of course, essential for rolling out the pastry dough. A thick, heavy, wooden one will do the job well. When rolling, always ensure that the pastry is cold and lightly flour the rolling pin rather than the pastry. This will stop you from adding too much flour to the pastry (which will make it dry and crumbly) and will prevent the rolling pin sticking to the pastry surface. Roll out your pastry using gentle strokes to avoid overstretching it (which will make it tough). Always chill shortcrust pastry before rolling, even if only for a short time. This will allow the gluten to 'relax' and helps prevent the pastry from shrinking when it is cooked.

quantities and sizes

When a recipe calls for 10oz of pastry this means that it should be made with 7oz of flour. This is because the weight of the pastry also includes the weight of the fat (so pastry made with 10oz of flour really weighs in at 15oz).

7oz flour = 10oz pastry · 10oz flour = 15oz pastry · 13oz flour = 1¼lb pastry

single-crust pie

10oz pastry covers a 1 pint dish · 14oz pastry covers a 2½–3½ pint dish · 1¼lb pastry covers a 4 pint dish

double-crust pie

10oz pastry lines and covers an 7in dish · 15oz pastry lines and covers a 9in dish · 1¼lb pastry lines and covers a 12in dish

shortcrust pastry

This is a great all-purpose plain pastry which is robust and easy to handle. The proportions to remember are half fat to flour, with enough liquid to combine. I've tried other quantities but I always end up coming back to this pastry mantra and it works perfectly every time. This is the simplest and most widely used pastry and is suitable for either sweet or savory pies. The mixture of butter and lard or shortening really is the best combination for flavor and texture, producing a light, crisp texture and delicious, buttery taste. If you don't want to use real lard simply substitute a white vegetable fat shortening—you will find a whole selection to choose from. When making a sweet pie, add 2 tablespoons of superfine sugar to the dough mix.

makes 10oz/300g of pastry
1³/₄ cups/200g plain flour · pinch salt · ¹/₂ stick/50g butter · ¹/₄ cup/50g lard or shortening
2–3 tbsp water, to mix

Sift the flour and salt into a bowl. Cut the fat into cubes and add this to the flour. Use your fingertips to rub the fat into the flour until the mixture resembles fine breadcrumbs. Add the water very gradually, stirring it in with a knife. When the dough just sticks together, knead it lightly until it forms a ball. Wrap in plastic wrap and allow to rest for at least 15 minutes in the refrigerator. It can be left in the refrigerator for up to 2 days. Alternatively it can be frozen until ready to use.

Once you have the basic mixture you can flavor it with toasted ground spices, chopped fresh herbs or toasted and finely chopped nuts.

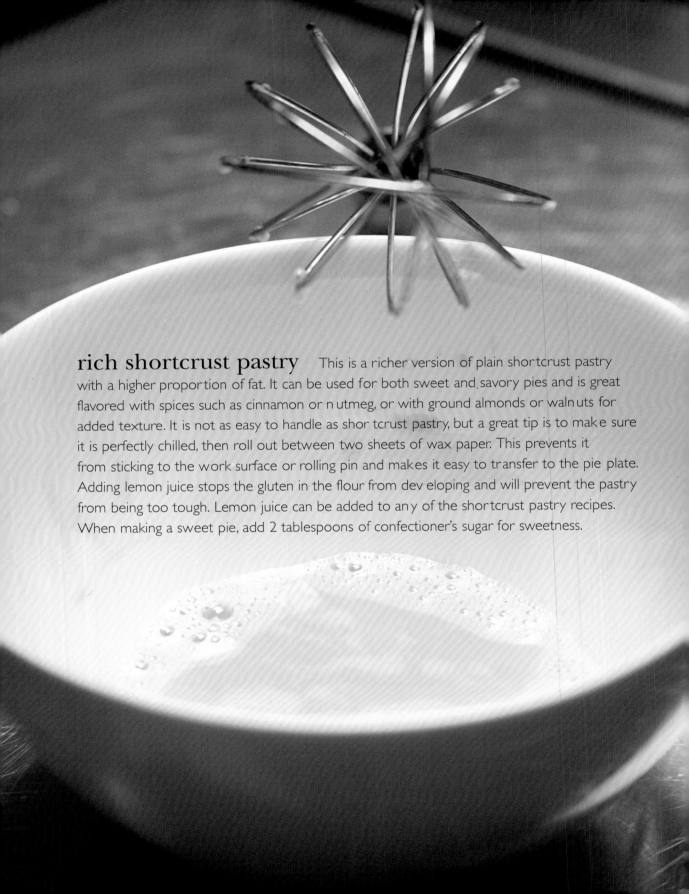

rich shortcrust pastry

This is a richer version of plain shortcrust pastry with a higher proportion of fat. It can be used for both sweet and savory pies and is great flavored with spices such as cinnamon or nutmeg, or with ground almonds or walnuts for added texture. It is not as easy to handle as shortcrust pastry, but a great tip is to make sure it is perfectly chilled, then roll out between two sheets of wax paper. This prevents it from sticking to the work surface or rolling pin and makes it easy to transfer to the pie plate. Adding lemon juice stops the gluten in the flour from developing and will prevent the pastry from being too tough. Lemon juice can be added to any of the shortcrust pastry recipes. When making a sweet pie, add 2 tablespoons of confectioner's sugar for sweetness.

makes 10oz/300g of pastry
$1^3/4$ cups/200g plain flour · $^1/4$ tsp salt · 2 tbsp icing sugar, if making sweet pastry · 100g/$3^1/2$oz
$^3/4$ stick plus 1 tbsp/100g unsalted butter, cold · 1 egg, beaten · 1 tsp lemon juice · 2 tbsp iced water

Sift together the flour and salt (and confectioner's sugar, if making sweet pastry). Cut the butter into cubes and add half of it to the flour. Gently and swiftly rub the fat into the flour until it resembles coarse breadcrumbs. Add the rest of the butter and mix until it's the size of small peas. Make a well in the center with your fist. Mix the beaten egg with the lemon juice and water and gradually pour into the well a little at a time, using a knife to mix the dough as you go. If the mixture looks like it has sufficient liquid to form a dough, don't add all the liquid as the absorbency of flours varies. Turn out on to a floured board and knead lightly until smooth. Shape into a ball, wrap in plastic wrap and refrigerate for at least 30 minutes before use.

cheese pastry
This is great for enriching savory pies but also works beautifully for sweet fruit pies too, such as the Apple Pie on page 154. You can experiment with different cheeses for this pastry, but ones with a strong flavor such as Red Leicester, Parmesan, mature Cheddar, and Gruyère work best. Add a pinch of mustard powder for extra oomph.

makes 13oz of pastry
$1^3/4$ cups/200g all-purpose flour · pinch salt · $1^1/4$ sticks/150g butter · $^1/2$ cup/50g grated hard cheese, such as mature Cheddar or Parmesan · 2–3 tbsp water, to mix

Sift the flour and salt in a bowl. Cut the fat into pieces and add this to the flour. Use your fingertips to rub the fat into the flour until the mixture resembles fine breadcrumbs. Stir in the cheese, then add the water very gradually, stirring it in with a knife. When the dough just sticks together, knead it lightly into a ball, wrap in plastic wrap and allow it to rest for at least 15 minutes in the refrigerator.

flaky and puff pastries

It's quite tricky and time-consuming to make these rich flaky crusts, which is why most people resort to the simpler alternative of buying ready-made. These are now of a very high standard, so I've given recipes only for the simpler types of flaky and puff pastry. The very high fat content of puff pastry is what makes it rich and fine, but can also cause it to be difficult to handle. As with all pastry crusts, though, a little practice will make perfect.

It is the rolling and folding procedure that ensures the fat and flour remain in layers, giving a crisp flaky crust.

flaky pastry

This is a wonderful pastry to make if you're pulling out all the stops. If you've spent a lot of time, effort, and perhaps money creating a fantastic filling for a pie, then it only makes sense to finish it off with a wonderful topping. Obviously this is not one for everyday pies. When baked, the crust looks a little like puff pastry but has fewer layers. The fat is incorporated by dotting it over the rolled-out dough. This creates pockets of air and helps to separate the layers.

makes 13oz of pastry
2 cups/225g all-purpose flour · 1/4 tsp salt · 3/4 stick/75g butter, softened
1/4 cup + 2 tbsp/75g shortening, softened · 2/3 cup/150ml water · 1 tsp lemon juice

First sift the flour with the salt. In a large bowl mix together the softened butter and shortening and divide into four equal portions. Rub one of these portions into the flour and mix to a soft dough with the water and lemon juice.

Roll this pastry into an oblong three times as long as it is wide measuring 12 x 4in/30 x 10cm. Dot another quarter of the fat over the top two-thirds of the rolled-out pastry. Fold the bottom third up and the top third down. Turn the dough sideways. Press down the edges of the pastry to seal the fat inside. Roll out again and repeat this procedure until all the fat is used up. Leave the pastry to rest for 5 minutes between each turn. Wrap in plastic wrap and leave to chill in the refrigerator for at least 30 minutes.

When ready to use, roll out to 1/4in/3mm thick. Should the pastry become warm and sticky at any time, wrap it in plastic wrap and chill for about 15 minutes before continuing.

short cut flaky pastry

This is so easy to make and gives really great results—you just have to be a bit organized and get the butter in the freezer in advance. In this version, instead of dotting the dough with the fat, you can grate or shred it into the flour. The resulting pastry crust has the same buttery flavor and crispness as flaky pastry but is not as light.

makes 14¹/4oz of pastry
2 sticks/200g butter · 2¹/2 cups/350g all-purpose flour · pinch salt · 6 tbsp ice water

Place the butter in the freezer for about 20 minutes until it is very hard. Sift the flour and salt into a mixing bowl. Hold the butter using a piece of baking parchment paper or kitchen foil and grate it into the flour, working quickly. Stir the butter and flour together, sprinkle with water, and mix to make a dough, adding a little more water if needed. Wrap in plastic wrap and chill for about 30 minutes before using.

rough puff pastry

Compared to flaky and puff pastry, this is much more straightforward and I would recommend it for rich pies such as game and venison. The end result is well worth it and incredibly satisfying.

makes about 400g/13oz of pastry
200g/7oz plain flour · 1/4 tsp salt · 75g/3oz butter · 75g/3oz lard or white vegetable fat
100ml/3 1/2fl oz cold water · 1 tsp lemon juice

Mix together the flour and salt. Cut both the fats into small cubes (this is where it differs from flaky pastry). Mix the fat into the flour without breaking up the lumps. Mix to a stiff dough with the water and lemon juice.

On a floured board, roll the dough into a strip three times as long as it is wide – about 30 x 10cm/12 x 4in. Fold the top third down and bottom third up. Turn the pastry sideways and seal the edges. Continue to roll and fold four times altogether. Leave the pastry to rest for 15 minutes between each folding and rolling. Wrap in cling film and leave to rest and chill in the fridge for 30 minutes before using.

potato pastry

This is a substantial pastry with a really crumbly texture when baked. Roll it out quite thickly and use it as a single crust on chunky meat pies.

makes 400g/13oz of pastry
100g/3 1/2oz floury potatoes, peeled and diced · 100g/3 1/2oz butter, diced · 200g/7oz plain flour
1 egg, beaten

Cook the diced potatoes in a pan of salted water until tender. Drain well and mash until smooth. Now rub the butter into the flour until the mixture resembles fine breadcrumbs. Mix together the beaten egg and a little water and stir into the mashed potato. Add to the flour mixture and stir with a round-bladed knife to form a smooth, pliable dough. Wrap in cling film and chill in the fridge for about 30 minutes before using.

wholemeal pastry

This pastry is best made with half plain and half wholemeal flour as wholemeal flour has a high proportion of coarse bran and is a little too heavy and tough when used alone for pastry. Add the water carefully, as wholemeal flour can take up a good deal of moisture and adding too much water can make the pastry very hard and crisp.

makes 10oz of pastry
1 cup/100g whole wheat flour · 1 cup/100g all-purpose flour · pinch mustard powder · pinch salt
1 stick/100g butter · 2–3 tbsp ice water, to mix

Mix together the flours, mustard powder, and salt. Cut the fat into cubes and add this to the flour.
Use your fingertips to rub the fat into the flour until the mixture resembles fine breadcrumbs. Add the
water very gradually, stirring it in with a knife. When the dough just sticks together, knead it lightly into
a ball. Wrap in plastic wrap and allow to rest for at least 15 minutes in the refrigerator before use.

hot-water crust   This pastry gets its name from the hot water which is added to make
a malleable dough strong enough to hold the filling. It is used for making raised pies such as pork
pies, raised game pies, and Scotch pies. The addition of just a little confectioner's sugar increases the
richness of the pastry without adding sweetness.

makes about 1lb of pastry
3¹/₂ cups/450g all-purpose flour · ¹/₂ tsp salt · 1 tbsp confectioner's sugar · 1 egg, beaten
³/₄ cup/200ml water · ³/₄ stick/80g butter · ¹/₄ cup + 2 tbsp or ³/₄ stick/80g lard

Mix the flour, salt, and confectioner's sugar in a large bowl. Make a dip in the middle, pour in the egg and toss
a liberal covering of flour over the egg. Put the water, butter, and lard into a saucepan and bring slowly to a
boil. When the liquid boils, pour it on to the flour, mixing with a knife as you go. Knead until all the egg
streaks have gone and the pastry is smooth. Use immediately to make your pie because when the pastry
cools it will harden and become unmanageable. (NB Lard is better than shortening for hot-water crust
pastry.)

wheat-free pastry

This is a recipe that I have used again and again and in my experience works really well. The problem with a wheat-free pastry is trying to achieve the same stretchy consistency you get with wheat pastry. It is the gluten in wheat flour which gives the pastry its texture. A solution to this is to add xanthan gum, which is readily available in health-food shops. This is a white powder which, when mixed with nonwheat flours and liquid, makes the pastry stretchy and easy to roll out. Gluten-free flour is also now fairly widely available. It can make the dough crumbly and difficult to roll, but with patience it will prove a great substitute.

makes 10oz of pastry

1/2 cup/75g rice flour · 1/2 cup/75g fine cornmeal (polenta) · 1/2 cup/75g potato flour · pinch salt
1 1/4 sticks/150g butter, cut into cubes · 1 egg · 2 tbsp ice water · 1 tsp xanthan gum

Place the rice flour, cornmeal, potato flour, and salt in a bowl and mix together well. Add the butter to the dry ingredients and carefully rub together with your fingertips until the mixture resembles breadcrumbs. Mix the egg with the water and xanthan gum and add to the flour and butter a little at a time. You might find that the mixture comes together to make a dough before you have added all the liquid; this is fine— don't be tempted to add it all, as flours have different levels of absorbency. Tip the dough out onto a lightly floured surface and knead for a few minutes until silky smooth. Wrap in plastic wrap and refrigerate for 30 minutes until ready to use. Use as for shortcrust pastry.

food processor pastry

If you happen to have a food processor, this method for making pastry is great for speed and ease. It is particularly good for rich pastry and sweet pastry, where the higher proportions of fat and sugar can make the dough difficult to handle with warm hands. A food processor ensures that the dough stays cool.

makes 10oz of pastry

2 cups/225g all-purpose flour · pinch salt · 2 tbsp superfine sugar, if making sweet shortcrust
1/2 stick/50g butter, cut into cubes · 1/2 stick/50g lard or 1/4 cup shortening, cut into cubes
2–3 tbsp water, to mix

Place the flour and salt (and sugar if making sweet shortcrust) in the food processor and process for 4–5 seconds. Scatter the cubes of butter and lard or shortening over the dry ingredients. Process for 10 seconds only, or until the mixture resembles fine breadcrumbs. Sprinkle the water over the flour mixture and use the pulse button to process until the dough starts to hold together. It should feel neither too dry nor too wet. Remove the mixture from the processor and form it into a ball. Lightly knead on a floured surface for a few seconds until smooth, then wrap in plastic wrap and chill for 30 minutes before using.

trouble shooting

faults in shortcrust pastry

Soggy bottom pastry   This may occur if your filling contains too much liquid. Your pie dish may also be too thick and not conduct the heat to the pastry efficiently. The oven may not be hot enough, or the pie may have been placed too high in the oven and cooked too quickly. Make sure the oven is at the right temperature and bake the pie on a preheated baking sheet. The filling needs to be refrigerator-cold or it will begin to steam the pastry and make it go soggy before you bake it.

Pastry shrinks when cooked   Because pastry is tense after being rolled out, it needs to relax in the refrigerator for at least 30 minutes before cooking. Placing the dough in the freezer, to take it from relaxed to super-chilled, can prevent shrinkage. Roll out gently and don't overstretch the pastry.

Pastry is crumbly and hard to handle   Adding too much fat and overmixing or adding too little liquid can make pastry crumbly. It is vital to weigh ingredients carefully and handle the dough gently.

Cooked pastry is tough   This occurs when too little fat and too much liquid are added. Be careful not to overhandle the dough and make sure the oven is hot.

faults in flaky and puff pastries

Pastry hard and tough   Too much water has been added to the flour but not enough fat. It is important to keep the pastry cool during rolling and the oven needs to be hot.

Pastry not risen   The fat may have been too warm and has blended with the flour instead of remaining in layers. Make sure you rest the pastry sufficiently between rollings.

Pastry soggy in the middle   This is a result of the pastry being undercooked. Don't place the pastry on too high a shelf in the oven.

faults in hot-water crust pastry

Pastry won't mold   The fat and water may have been too cold when added to the flour, or you have used insufficient fat and water.

Crust bursts during cooking   The crust may have been unevenly molded, making some parts thinner than others.

Crust collapses when removed from mold   The pastry could be too warm and too thin. Ensure that the pastry is chilled before removing from the mold before baking.

homepie

Comforting, tasty, and satisfying, home pies made with love are the perfect solution to a cold wintry day, feeding a hungry family, or making a special treat for friends.

No one could resist a deep, single-crusted, juicy, and tender meat pie served in an earthenware dish and topped with light flaky or puff pastry. Or a simple double-crusted pie baked in a pie plate which you can cut and come back to again and again. These are the pies we love to eat with family and friends, and investing just a little time and attention will allow you to produce something that will impress every time.

If you use good-quality ingredients and leave enough time for slow cooking, everything else will be pretty straightforward. Sit back and enjoy everyone's delight as the decisive moment arrives and you cut into the pie, releasing an archetypal puff of steam and the divine aroma.

This recipe came from my friend David Herbert, who developed it after overcooking lamb shanks and rescuing them by putting them into a pie.

braised lamb shank pie

The lamb in this pie cooks down until it is incredibly tender, falling apart to make a succulent filling. It deserves to be topped by a rich, puff pastry lid. The shanks are cut from the narrow end of the leg joint.

serves 6

for the pastry
13oz puff pastry (see page 20) · beaten egg, to glaze

for the filling
$^{1}/_{2}$ cup/50g all-purpose flour · 6 lamb shanks · 2 tbsp olive oil · 4 red onions, quartered
8 cloves garlic, peeled · 1 bottle full-bodied red wine · 1$^{1}/_{4}$ cups/300ml beef stock
2 tbsp finely chopped rosemary · 3 tbsp redcurrant jelly · salt and ground black pepper

Season the flour with a good pinch of salt and plenty of ground black pepper. Dust the shanks in the seasoned flour. Heat the oil in a large saucepan or heavy-bottomed flameproof casserole dish and brown the shanks all over. Add any remaining flour, the onions, and garlic and stir well. Pour in the wine, stock, rosemary, redcurrant jelly, and a good grinding of black pepper.

Bring to a boil, cover, and turn down the heat to cook at a very gentle simmer for about 2 hours until the meat falls off the bone and the sauce is rich and thickened. Remove the bones from the pan, reserving three of them, and flake the meat into small pieces.

Preheat the oven to 400°F.

Fill an 8 cup/2 litre pie dish with the lamb filling. Roll out the pastry to about $^{1}/_{8}$in/3mm thick and about 1in/2.5cm larger than the dish. Cut a $^{3}/_{4}$in/2cm strip from the pastry. Brush the rim of the dish with a little water and place the pastry strip around the rim, pressing it down. Sit the 3 reserved lamb bones in the pie filling at intervals along the length of the dish. These will act as pie funnels, releasing the steam when the pie is baking, and will also stop the pastry from sinking into the filling and becoming soggy. Cut 3 slits in the remaining pastry at the same intervals as the lamb bones. Place the pastry lid over the top and slide it over the bones. Press down the edges of the pastry to seal. Trim off any excess pastry and crimp the edges with a fork or between your thumb and fore-finger. Brush with beaten egg and bake for 30–35 minutes until the pastry is crisp and golden.

steak and kidney pie

It's so difficult to give a recipe for this most famous of pies as opinions on the definitive version vary widely. However, the theme they all seem to share is a long, slow cooking time for the meat, to give a rich, dark stew with a glossy gravy. They also all agree that the filling tastes best when made up to two days ahead and that a deep earthenware dish should be used for the pie and a good puff or flaky pastry for the lid. My butcher reckons that the best cut of meat for slow cooking is chuck steak, which creates a wonderful gravy, and that pigs' kidneys provide the best flavor.

serves 6

for the pastry
13oz flaky pastry (see page 19) · beaten egg, to glaze

for the filling
3$^{1}/_{2}$ tbsp/25g all-purpose flour · 2lb/900g chuck steak, cut into 1in/2.5cm cubes · $^{1}/_{2}$lb/225g pigs' kidneys, cut into 1in/2.5cm cubes · $^{1}/_{4}$ stick/25g butter · 2 large onions, finely sliced · 1 tbsp chopped fresh thyme · 5oz/150g cremini mushrooms, roughly chopped · 1$^{1}/_{4}$ cups/300ml red wine 1$^{1}/_{4}$ cups/300ml beef stock · 2 tbsp Worcestershire sauce · salt and ground black pepper

Preheat the oven to 350°F.

Sift the flour into a large plastic bag and add the steak and kidneys. Season with a little salt and plenty of ground black pepper. Shake well until the meat is completely coated with flour.

Heat the butter in a large, heavy-bottomed flameproof casserole dish and cook the onions until just softened but not browned. Add the meat, thyme, and mushrooms and brown the meat quickly on all sides. Add any leftover flour and pour in the wine, stock, and Worcestershire sauce. Bring to a boil, cover and place in the oven for 1$^{1}/_{2}$ hours until the meat is tender and the gravy thick and glossy. Transfer the meat and gravy into an 8 cup/2 litre deep pie dish and leave to cool.

Increase the oven temperature to 400°F.

Roll out the pastry to a thickness of about $^{1}/_{8}$in/3mm. Cut a $^{3}/_{4}$in/2cm strip from the rolled-out pastry. Brush the rim of the pie dish with water and place the pastry strip around the rim, pressing it down. Cut out the remaining pastry about 1in/2.5cm larger than the dish. Sit a pie funnel in the center of the filling to support the pastry and stop it from sinking into the filling and becoming soggy. Place the pastry lid over the top of the filling and press down the edges to seal. Trim off any excess pastry and crimp the edges with a fork, or between your thumb and index finger. Brush the top of the pie with beaten egg and make a hole in the center to reveal the pie funnel. Bake for 30–35 minutes until the pastry is crisp and golden.

steak and oyster pie
This old-fashioned recipe was a Victorian favorite. Oysters replace kidneys to give the gravy a slight taste of the sea—it sounds a little mad but, believe me, it makes the most delicious filling for a pie. This recipe is best made as individual pies.

Buy 8 fresh rock oysters, open them and remove the flesh from the shells.
Simply prepare the Steak and Kidney Pie, as above, leaving out the kidneys. Spoon the cooled beef filling into 4 individual pie pans. Sit 2 rock oysters on the top of each pie filling. Roll out the pastry (as above) and cut out pie lids for the individual pies. Brush the edges of the pastry with beaten egg, lay over the filling and press the edges on to the rims of the pans. Cut a slit in the middle of each lid and brush with beaten egg. Rest in the refrigerator for 30 minutes then bake in a preheated oven at 400°F for 30 minutes until the pastry is golden.

rabbit pot pie with polenta crust

Rabbit pies have been made in many different ways over the centuries. Generally the meat is cooked first, then placed in an earthenware pot sealed with a pastry lid to keep in the flavor. I've used this method here to create a really wonderful, tasty pie. The pastry is simply draped over the top of the dish, making it a very simple pie to prepare, but it both looks and tastes very impressive. When making the filling, bear in mind that wild rabbit has a much stronger flavor and needs a little more cooking time than the farmed variety.

serves 4

for the pastry
10oz/300g shortcrust pastry (see page 15), ¹/₂ cup/50g of the flour replaced with coarse polenta beaten egg, to glaze · 4 tbsp grated Parmesan cheese

for the filling
¹/₄ stick/25g butter · 1 rabbit, cut into pieces · 4oz/100g piece pancetta, diced · 1 onion, finely chopped · 2 tbsp all-purpose flour · 1¹/₄ cups/300ml white wine · ²/₃ cup/150ml heavy cream 4 cloves garlic, bruised · 2 sprigs rosemary · salt and ground black pepper

Heat the butter in a large skillet and cook the rabbit pieces until browned (cook it in batches if necessary). Remove from the skillet, add the pancetta and cook for 4 minutes until golden. Add the onion and cook for 4 minutes until the onion has softened.

Add the flour and stir for 1 minute, then add the white wine and simmer rapidly. Stir in the cream and garlic and season with a little salt and plenty of ground black pepper. Return the rabbit to the skillet with a sprig of rosemary and simmer on a very low heat for 20–25 minutes until the sauce has reduced and thickened.

Preheat the oven to 400°F.

Spoon the mix into 1 large or 4 individual earthenware pie dishes and roll out the pastry to fit the top, allowing it to drape over the edges. Brush with beaten egg, sprinkle with Parmesan and leaves from the remaining rosemary sprig. Bake for 30 minutes.

venison pie with thyme, mustard, and shallots

This wonderful pie has a rich and flavorsome filling and deserves the perfect flaky crust. The large amount of mustard gives a real depth of flavor and a wonderful creamy texture. It's certainly not an everyday dinner.

serves 6

for the pastry
14¹/₂oz/450g short-cut flaky pastry (see page 19) · beaten egg, to glaze

for the filling
1¹/₂oz/40g dried wild mushrooms · 3¹/₂ tbsp/25g all-purpose flour · 1 tbsp fresh thyme
2lb/1kg diced venison · 2 tbsp olive oil · 13oz/400g shallots, peeled and left whole
2 cloves garlic, chopped · 2 tbsp dark brown sugar · 2 cups/500ml dark beer
1¹/₄ cups/300ml beef stock · 2 tbsp Worcestershire sauce · 2 tbsp Dijon mustard
salt and ground black pepper

Place the mushrooms in a small bowl and pour over boiling water to soak. Set aside while you prepare the rest of the filling.

Sift the flour into a large plastic bag, add the thyme and season with a little salt and a good grinding of black pepper. Add the diced venison and shake well to coat all the pieces.

Heat 1 tablespoon of the oil in a deep, flameproof casserole and fry the shallots for 4–5 minutes until beginning to color and soften. Add the garlic and toss with the shallots over a medium heat for a minute. Remove from the casserole and set aside.

Add the remaining oil to the casserole and brown one batch of venison on all sides, remove and set aside. Repeat with the remaining venison. Return all the meat to the casserole along with the fried shallots and garlic. Stir in the brown sugar and heat through for a few minutes. Stir in the dark beer and beef stock, the Worcestershire sauce, Dijon mustard, mushrooms, and about ¹/₃ cup/100ml of the soaking liquid from the mushrooms. Season and bring gently to a boil. Cover and simmer gently for 2 hours until the meat is tender and the sauce is glossy and thickened. Spoon into an 8 cup/2 litre deep pie dish and set aside to cool completely.

Preheat the oven to 400°F.

Roll out the pastry to a thickness of about ¹/₈in/3mm. Cut a ³/₄in/2cm strip from the rolled-out pastry. Brush the rim of the pie dish with water and place the pastry strip around the rim, pressing it down. Cut out a lid from the remaining pastry about 1in/2.5cm larger than the dish. Sit a pie funnel into the center of the filling to support the pastry and stop it from sinking into the filling and becoming soggy. Place the pastry lid over the top and press down on the edges to seal. Trim off any excess pastry and crimp the edges with a fork, or between your thumb and index finger. Brush the top with beaten egg and make a hole in the center to reveal the pie funnel. Use the pastry trimmings to make decorations for the surface of the pie. Bake for 30–35 minutes until the pastry is crisp and golden.

beef and ale pie

A classic rich and flavorsome home pie. The addition of beer, such as Guiness or dark beer, gives a real richness to the sauce. It is even better if you make the filling the day before, so that the stew has time to thicken up a little and the flavors can really develop. It is crying out for mash.

serves 4–6

for the pastry
300g/10oz rich shortcrust pastry (see page 16) · beaten egg, to glaze

for the filling
3½lb tbsp all-purpose flour · 2lb/900g chuck steak, cut into 1in/2.5cm cubes · 2 tbsp butter
1 tbsp vegetable oil · 2 large onions, thinly sliced · 2 carrots, chopped into 1in/2.5cm cubes
2 tsp Worcestershire sauce · 2 tsp tomato paste · 2 cups/500ml Guinness or dark beer
1¼ cups/300ml hot beef stock · 2 tsp sugar · salt and ground black pepper

Place the flour in a large bowl and season with salt and ground black pepper, add the cubes of meat and toss well in the flour until evenly coated.

Heat the butter and oil in a large, heavy-based, flameproof casserole until the butter has melted. Add the meat to the fat in batches and brown all over for just a minute, then remove with a slotted spoon and set aside. Add the onions and carrots to the casserole and fry gently for about 2 minutes, then return the meat to the pan with the Worcestershire sauce, tomato paste, beer, stock, and sugar. Grind in plenty of black pepper and add a little salt, stir well and bring to the boil. Cover, reduce to a simmer and cook slowly for 2 hours until the meat is tender and the sauce is thick and glossy. Remove from the heat, place into a 6 cup/1.5 litre deep pie dish and leave to cool completely.

Preheat the oven to 400°F.

Roll out the pastry to a thickness of about/1/8in/3mm. Cut a ¾in/2cm strip from the rolled-out pastry. Brush the rim of the pie dish with water and place the pastry strip around the rim, pressing it down. Cut out the remaining pastry about 1in/2.5cm larger than the dish. Sit a pie funnel in the center of the filling; it will support the pastry and stop it sinking into the filling and becoming soggy. Place the pastry lid over the top and press down on to the edges to seal. Trim off any excess pastry and crimp the edges with a fork, or between your thumb and forefinger. Brush the top with beaten egg and make a hole in the centre to reveal the funnel. Bake for 30–35 minutes until the pastry is crisp and golden.

meat and potato pie

This has got to be the definitive pie—loved or hated, it is eaten up and down Britain as a ready-made hand-held pie or as a tray-baked school dinner. When made with good-quality ground steak and the right mixture of flavorings and pastry crust, it is delicious and one of the truly great pies. It requires a large amount of pastry as it is a double-crusted pie. My recipe is in the tray-baked family tradition; serve it with extra gravy, peas, and mashed potato for the ultimate dinner *(illustrated on preceding pages)*.

serves 6

for the pastry
1lb/500g shortcrust pastry (see page 15) · 2 tbsp milk, to glaze

for the filling
1 tbsp olive oil · 1 onion, finely chopped · 1 clove garlic, crushed · 1¹/₂lb/700g good-quality coarse-ground beef · 2 tbsp all-purpose flour · ³/₄ cup/200ml beef stock · 2 tbsp tomato paste 2 tbsp savory brown sauce · 2 large potatoes, peeled and cubed · salt and ground black pepper

Preheat the oven to 400°F. Place a baking sheet in the oven to heat.

Heat the oil in a large saucepan. Add the onion and cook gently for a few minutes until beginning to soften. Add the garlic and ground beef and cook for about 5 minutes until the meat is browned all over. Stir in the flour, toss with the beef, and cook for a couple of minutes.

Add the beef stock, tomato paste, savory brown sauce, and cubed potatoes and simmer gently for about 10 minutes until thickened slightly. Season well to taste and leave to cool.

Roll out half of the pastry and use to line a roasting pan or dish measuring 14 × 10in/35 × 25cm. Spoon the cooled filling mixture on to the pastry. Roll out the remaining pastry and place on top, pressing the edges together to seal. Crimp the edges using your fingertips and brush the top with a little milk to glaze. Place on the baking sheet and bake for 35–40 minutes until golden.

lamb, mint, and pumpkin pie

What a wonderful pie—a perfect combination of flavors topped with toasted cumin pastry.

serves 6

for the pastry
13oz/400g shortcrust pastry (see page 15), with 2 tsp toasted
cumin seeds added to the mixture · beaten egg, to glaze

for the filling
4 tbsp olive oil · 2lb/1kg boned shoulder of lamb, trimmed
and cut into 1in/2.5cm cubes · 2 cups/500ml dark beer
2 large onions, chopped · 2 cloves garlic, chopped · 2 celery
stalks, chopped · 2 bay leaves · large bunch mint, chopped
1 x 28oz can/2 x 400g cans chopped tomatoes · 1 large red
chili · 1 large butternut squash, peeled and chopped into
1in/2.5cm cubes · salt and ground black pepper

Preheat the oven to 350°F.

Heat the olive oil in an 8 cup/2 litre heavy-based flameproof casserole and fry the lamb until browned
all over. Add the beer, onions, garlic, celery, and bay leaves, half the bunch of mint, the canned
tomatoes, and red chili. Season well to taste and cover. Place in the oven to bake for 1 1/2 hours.
Add the butternut squash and continue to cook for a further 1 hour until the meat is very tender.
Using a vegetable masher, press the butternut squash and mash it into the sauce to make a thick
gravy with the tender lamb. Stir in the remaining mint, spoon into an 8 cup/2 litre deep pie dish
and leave to cool.

Increase the oven temperature to 400°F.

Roll out the pastry to a thickness of about 1/8in/3mm. Cut a 3/4in/2cm strip from the rolled-out
pastry. Brush the rim of the pie dish with water and place the pastry strip around the rim, pressing
it down. Cut out a lid from the remaining pastry about 1in/2.5cm larger than the dish. Sit a pie
funnel into the center of the filling to support the pastry and stop it from sinking into the filling and
becoming soggy. Place the pastry lid over the top and press down on to the edges to seal. Trim off
any excess pastry and crimp the edges with a fork, or between your thumb and forefinger. Brush
the pastry with beaten egg and make a hole in the center to reveal the pie funnel. Use the pastry
trimmings to make decorations for the surface of the pie. Bake for 30–35 minutes until the pastry
is crisp and golden.

game pie

As game meat can be quite unpredictable in its tenderness (which affects its cooking time), I poach the pheasant before adding it to the pie because this ensures that the meat is perfectly succulent. Also, you then have the wonderful game stock which can be used to make the delicious sauce for the pie. This is another special-occasion pie which deserves a perfect crust.

serves 6

for the pastry
13oz/400g puff pastry (see page 20) · beaten egg, to glaze

for the filling

4 prepared pheasants · 3 onions · I carrot · 2 celery stalks · 4 black peppercorns
3¹/₂ tbsp/25g all-purpose flour · ¹/₂lb/225g lean chuck steak, cut into ³/₄in/2cm cubes
4oz/115g smoked bacon strips, cut into pieces · 2 tbsp butter · I large clove garlic, finely chopped
I tbsp tomato paste · small bunch chopped parsley · 2 tbsp redcurrant jelly · 3¹/₂oz/100g
cremini mushrooms, sliced small pinch grated nutmeg · salt and ground black pepper

Place the pheasants in a large saucepan and cover with water. Add I of the onions (whole), carrot, celery, and peppercorns and bring to a boil. Simmer for I hour or until the pheasants are tender. Remove the pheasants from the stock and leave to cool. Return the stock to the heat and continue to simmer until reduced by half, then set aside. Remove the pheasant meat from the carcasses and chop roughly.

Sift the flour into a large plastic bag with some salt and black pepper. Add the chuck steak and shake well to coat it in the flour.

Heat a heavy skillet and cook the bacon for a few minutes until it releases its fat. Add the butter and when it has melted add the chuck steak and cook for about 4 minutes until browned all over. Chop the remaining onions and add to the skillet with the garlic. Cook for a further few minutes, then pour in 1¹/₄ cups/300ml of the reduced pheasant stock. Add the tomato paste, parsley, redcurrant jelly, and the mushrooms. Season to taste and add the nutmeg. Cover and simmer gently for 30 minutes. Add the chopped pheasant to the skillet, then transfer to an 8 cup/2 litre deep pie dish and set aside to cool.

Preheat the oven to 400°F.

Roll out the pastry to a thickness of about ¹/₈in/3mm. Cut a ³/₄in/2cm strip from the rolled-out pastry. Brush the rim of the pie dish with water and place the pastry strip around the rim, pressing it down. Cut out a lid from the remaining pastry about 1in/2.5cm larger than the dish. Sit a pie funnel into the center of the filling to support the pastry and stop it from sinking into the filling and becoming soggy. Place the pastry lid over the top and press down on the edges to seal. Trim off any excess pastry and crimp the edges with a fork, or between your thumb and index finger. Brush the top with beaten egg and make a hole in the center to reveal the pie funnel. Use the pastry trimmings to make decorations for the top of the pie.

Bake for 30–35 minutes until the pastry is crisp and golden.

deep egg and bacon pie

This is rather like the classic quiche Lorraine with a pastry lid. You really can't go wrong with the combination of egg, bacon, cheese, and onion. This deep pie is cooked in a loose-bottomed cake pan so it can be easily cut into wedges, making it perfect for picnics. I have no problem eating it for breakfast, though!

serves 6

for the pastry
13oz/400g rich shortcrust pastry (see page 16) · beaten egg, to glaze

for the filling
10oz/300g lean pork, such as loin · 7oz/200g smoked bacon strips, rind removed
1 tbsp olive oil · 1 large onion, finely chopped · 2 cups/225g grated mature Cheddar cheese
1 clove garlic, crushed · bunch flat-leaf parsley, roughly chopped · bunch chives, chopped
2 eggs, lightly beaten · 4 tbsp crème fraîche or sour cream · salt and ground black pepper

Preheat the oven to 350°F.

Finely chop the pork and bacon and mix together. This can be done easily in a food processor but be careful not to over-process as the mixture can become too smooth. Heat the oil in a large saucepan and cook the onion for a few minutes. Add the pork and bacon and cook for about 5 minutes until lightly colored. Transfer to a bowl and leave to cool, then stir in the remaining ingredients, seasoning with a little salt and plenty of ground black pepper.

Roll out two-thirds of the pastry to a disk measuring about 12in/30cm across and drape into an approximately 8½in/22cm loose-bottomed cake pan to cover the bottom and the sides. Transfer the filling into the pie and brush the edges of the pastry with a little beaten egg. Roll out the remaining pastry to a smaller disk measuring approximately 9½in/24cm across and place over the top of the filled pie, pressing the edges together to seal. Trim away any excess pastry and brush the top of the pie with the rest of the beaten egg. Pierce the top with a fork to allow steam to escape. Place on a baking sheet and bake for 50–60 minutes until golden and crisp.

Allow to cool for about 10 minutes before removing it from the pan. Serve cut into wedges.

sausage, apple, and sage plate pie

Go to town with some really top-quality sausages to make this pie. I use a fine English sausage for this as it doesn't have an overpowering flavor and works well with the apple and sage. However, plain sausagemeat will also work well. Cook this pie in a shallow metal pan to ensure the base stays crispy.

serves 4

for the pastry
10oz/300g shortcrust pastry (see page 15) · beaten egg, to glaze

for the filling
1lb/450g good-quality English sausages or sausagemeat · 2 tbsp olive oil · 2 onions, finely sliced
1 tbsp wholegrain mustard · 1 tbsp chopped fresh sage · 2 small apples, peeled, cored, and
chopped · 2 tbsp crème fraîche or sour cream · salt and ground black pepper

Preheat the oven to 400°F.

Roll out about 6oz/175g of the pastry and use to line a shallow 9in/23cm pie plate. Roll out the
remaining pastry about 3/4in/2cm bigger than the pie plate and set aside.

Split the sausages, remove the skin and break up the meat into small pieces. Heat the oil in a large
skillet and gently cook the onions for about 8–10 minutes until softened. Add the sausagemeat and
cook for a further 5 minutes, stirring frequently until browned all over and breaking up the sausages
further with a wooden spoon during cooking. Remove from the heat and add the mustard, sage,
chopped apples, and crème fraîche or sour cream. Season with a little salt and ground black pepper
and mix well. Leave to cool.

Once the mixture has cooled, pile it into the center of the pie plate. Brush the edges of the pastry
with beaten egg and then top with the rolled-out lid, sealing the edges by pressing down well.
Trim off any excess pastry and crimp the edges with a fork, or between your thumb and index finger.
Brush with the remaining egg and make a hole or several slashes in the top to release the steam.

beef wellington

This pie is really one to go to town on with your pastry techniques. It is not necessarily a true pie, but in keeping with my definition of "any filling wrapped in pastry" it certainly fits the bill.

The method of cooking meat wrapped in pastry has a history that goes back to the eighteenth century and is a variation on the French classic *boeuf en croûte*. The English name was applied in 1815 in honor of the Duke of Wellington.

serves 6

for the pastry
1lb/500g ready-made puff pastry · beaten egg, to glaze

for the filling
2 tbsp/25g butter · 1 onion, finely chopped · 5oz/150g cremini mushrooms, finely chopped
2 cloves garlic, finely chopped · 3 tbsp chopped flat-leaf parsley · 4oz/100g smooth liver pâté
1³/₄lb/800g beef fillet · salt and ground black pepper

Melt the butter in a large skillet and cook the onion for about 5 minutes until beginning to soften. Add the mushrooms and cook for a further 5 minutes until soft and creamy. Stir in the garlic and parsley and season with a little salt and plenty of ground black pepper. Set aside to cool.

Beat the pâté into the mushroom mixture and set aside.

Preheat the oven to 400°F.

Roll out the puff pastry on a lightly floured surface to a sheet large enough to enclose the beef, reserving the scraps for decoration. Spread the pâté mixture down the middle of the pastry and lay the beef on top of the mixture. Brush the edges of the pastry with beaten egg and fold the pastry over the meat to enclose it in a neat package, sealing the edges well. Place the meat parcel onto a baking sheet, seam side down. Cut decorative leaves from the reserved pastry. Brush the package with beaten egg, decorate with the leaves, and chill for about 10 minutes.

Bake for 40–45 minutes until the crust is golden and puffed up. Transfer to a serving board and leave to stand for 10 minutes. Serve cut into thick slices.

russian fish pie

A Victorian and Edwardian favorite, this pie was adopted by the British from a Russian original known as *coulibiac*. Despite the fact that it has a pastry crust and is served hot, it resembles another famous import—kedgeree.

serves 6

for the pastry
1lb/500g ready-made puff pastry · beaten egg, to glaze

for the filling
1lb/500g salmon fillet · 1 1/4 cups/300ml milk · 3 black peppercorns · 1 bay leaf
1/2 cup/100g long-grain rice · 1/4 stick/25g butter · 1 onion, finely chopped · 4oz/100g mushrooms, thinly sliced · 4 hard-cooked eggs, sliced · pinch cayenne pepper · 2 tbsp chopped flat-leaf parsley · grated zest and juice 1 small lemon

Preheat the oven to 425°F.

Place the salmon in a large skillet with the milk, peppercorns, and bay leaf. Poach gently for about 5 minutes until the salmon is cooked through and flakes easily. Remove the salmon from the skillet and allow to cool; discard the milk.

Place the rice in a large saucepan of boiling water and cook for 10–12 minutes until tender. Drain and set aside. Heat the butter in a large saucepan and cook the onion for 5–6 minutes until tender. Add the mushrooms and cook for a further 5 minutes.

Place the cooked rice in a bowl and stir through the onion, mushrooms, hard-cooked eggs, cayenne pepper, parsley, salmon, lemon zest and juice, and plenty of salt and ground black pepper.

Roll out the pastry to a 16in/40cm square. Pile the filling in the center. Wet the corners of the pastry and fold them upward so that they meet and overlap slightly in the center to make an envelope shape. Press the joins together firmly and brush the pie all over with beaten egg.

Place on a large baking sheet and bake for 35–40 minutes until golden and puffed up.

the pie and mash shop

Eels, pie and mash are a combination particularly associated with London. Just after World War II, it was possible to consume pie and mash in at least 130 shops scattered all over the city. Today, only a fraction of the original eel, pie and mash houses remain and the majority are now situated in London's East End. Many people therefore believe this dish is an East End tradition.

The story begins in Victorian England, where the bustling streets were populated by piemen who walked miles each day selling meat, fish, and fruit

pies. These piemen provided many poor families with their only opportunity to buy hot food at a reasonable price. The meat pies were usually made from mutton or beef, the fruit pies consisted of apples, damsons, cherries, and currants and the fish pies were filled with eels.

Eels had become a popular dish for Londoners. They were usually accompanied by pea soup or parsley sauce, with chilies and vinegar added for spice. This parsley sauce is the famous "liquor" that is still served today. It is a basic recipe consisting of a thin white sauce with chopped parsley stirred in.

The first pie and mash shop was recorded in the late 1800s. It would have sold a variety of meat, eel and fruit pies, live eels, pea soup, and mashed potato. These shops heralded the end of the street piemen. A typical shop was fitted out with marble tables, wooden benches, white-tiled walls, and huge mirrors. Today, it is always an experience to dine in one of the few remaining outlets, which retain their original grandeur and are steeped in tradition and history. Even in cosmopolitan and ever-changing London, it is heartening that the pie and mash shop has managed to resist total obsolescence and you can still buy a very tasty homemade pie served with mash and gravy for a very reasonable price— a fact that will hopefully ensure the future of eels, pie and mash.

chicken, leek, and tarragon pie

It's difficult to single out the best chicken pie, but after many tried-and-tested combinations this has got to be my favorite. The tarragon and lemon provide a lovely touch of freshness.

serves 4–6

for the pastry
13oz/400g rich shortcrust pastry (see page 16) · beaten egg, to glaze

for the filling
3lb/1.5kg free-range chicken · 1 carrot, roughly chopped · 2 celery stalks, roughly chopped
2 onions, finely chopped · 4 sprigs tarragon · 1 tbsp olive oil · knob of butter
2 leeks, finely sliced · 2/3 cup/150ml white wine · 2 tbsp all-purpose flour
2/3 cup/150ml light cream · grated zest of 1/2 lemon · salt and ground black pepper

Place the chicken in a large saucepan with the carrot, celery, 1 of the onions and 3 tarragon sprigs. Season with a little salt and pepper and cover with water. Bring to a boil and simmer for 45 minutes until the chicken is cooked through. Remove the chicken from the pan and set aside to cool. Return the stock to the heat and simmer gently for a further 30 minutes until it is reduced by half.

Meanwhile heat the oil and butter in a large skillet, add the leeks and the remaining onion and gently cook for about 5 minutes until softened. Turn up the heat to high, add the wine and simmer rapidly for 3–4 minutes until reduced by half. Stir in the flour and mix well in the pan for 1 minute. Pour in the cream, about 2/3 cup/150ml of the reduced chicken stock and the lemon zest. Season with a little salt and plenty of ground black pepper.

Remove the meat from the cooled chicken carcass and chop or shred into small pieces. Add this and the remaining tarragon, chopped, to the leek and cream mixture and stir together. Set aside to cool.

Preheat the oven to 350°F. Place a baking sheet in the oven to heat.

Line the base of a 12 x 8in/30 x 20cm rectangular or 10¹/2in/26cm round pie pan with two-thirds of the pastry and fill with the chicken mixture. Brush the pastry edges with beaten egg. Roll out the remaining pastry to make a lid and lay over the filling, crimping the edges of the pastry with your fingertips to seal. Trim away any excess and brush with beaten egg to glaze. Place on the baking sheet and bake for 30–35 minutes until the crust is golden and crisp.

chicken, lemon, and oregano pie cooked in a skillet

The filling for this pie is based on *avgolemono*, a Greek sauce which is made from eggs and lemon. The recipe comes from my pal and fellow food writer Silvana Franco. She tops it with an oregano pastry, but if you are a bit pushed for time, ready-made short pastry will do just fine.

serves 6

for the pastry
10oz/300g shortcrust pastry (see page 15), with 1 tbsp dried oregano added to the dry mixture

for the filling
8 skinless, boneless chicken thighs, cut into 1in/2.5cm cubes · 1 tbsp all-purpose flour
2 tbsp olive oil, plus extra to glaze · 2¹/₂oz/70g pancetta, cubed · 2 large potatoes, peeled and cut into ³/₄in/2cm dice · 1 large onion, thinly sliced · 3 large egg yolks · grated zest and juice of 3 lemons · 2 cups/450ml warm chicken stock · 4 tbsp chopped fresh mint
salt and ground black pepper

Preheat the oven to 375°F.

Dust the chicken in the flour, shaking off the excess. Heat the oil in an approximately 9¹/₂in/24cm heavy-bottomed ovenproof skillet or oven- and flameproof dish. Add the chicken and pancetta and cook for about 5 minutes over a high heat until the chicken is nicely browned. Lift out the chicken and pancetta with a slotted spoon and set aside. Lower the heat, add the potatoes and onion and cook gently for 5–8 minutes until the onion is softened and golden.

In a large bowl, whisk together the egg yolks, lemon zest, and lemon juice. Slowly pour in the hot chicken stock, stirring continuously until the sauce is foamy and has thickened slightly. Season with salt and freshly ground pepper, then stir in the mint. Take the skillet off the heat and stir in the browned chicken and pancetta and the lemon sauce.

Roll out the pastry on a floured surface to make a circle a bit bigger than the skillet. Lay it on top of the skillet, roughly tucking the edges down the side of the skillet. Brush the top with olive oil and bake in the oven for 25–30 minutes until the pastry is dark golden.

greek spinach pie

This famous spinach and feta pie (*spanokopita*) is something so simple and sublime that I had to include it in the book. It looks tricky but, believe me, it really is straightforward to prepare – especially as wafer-thin phyllo pastry is widely available now. You may find that store-bought phyllo comes in various sizes, so adapt the recipe to fit.

serves 4

for the pastry
8 sheets ready-made phyllo pastry, measuring 10 x 9in/25 x 23cm

for the filling
1lb/500g spinach · 1 stick/100g butter · 1 large onion, finely chopped · 2 cloves garlic, chopped
1 3/4 cups/200g crumbled feta cheese · 2 tbsp pine nuts, toasted · 2 eggs, beaten
2 tbsp chopped fresh dill · 4 tbsp chopped flat-leaf parsley · salt and ground black pepper

Preheat the oven to 350°F.

Wash the spinach well. Place it in a large saucepan over low heat to cook down gently until completely wilted. Leave to cool, then drain well and squeeze out any excess liquid using your hands. Chop roughly.

Melt about 2 tablespoons of the butter in a skillet, add the onion, and cook for about 5 minutes until beginning to soften. Stir in the garlic and cook for a further minute. Remove from the heat and in a large bowl, combine the onion and garlic with the spinach, cheese, pine nuts, eggs, herbs, and seasoning to taste.

Melt the remaining butter. Arrange 1 sheet of phyllo pastry in the base of a shallow pan or ovenproof dish measuring about 8 1/2in/22cm square, allowing the edges of the pastry to overhang. Brush with melted butter, then arrange 3 more sheets on top, brushing each sheet as you go. Spoon the filling on top and spread out evenly. Fold the edges of the phyllo onto the spinach filling. Place another sheet of phyllo pastry on top of the spinach mixture and brush with melted butter. Arrange 3 more sheets of pastry on top, brushing each sheet as you go. Score the top lightly into squares and then bake for 20–25 minutes until golden brown. Serve hot or cold.

spanish pepper and chorizo pie

This is a hearty, family-sized pie, known as *empanada gallega*, which is eaten all over Spain in many variations. Its most popular fillings are always chorizo sausage, cured ham and pork with red bell peppers and onions.

The pastry crust is traditionally more like a pizza dough, but I have adapted it and topped the pie with a very simple shortcrust pastry streaked with saffron strands. It's a truly flavorsome pie and needs little accompaniment—just serve on its own with cold beer (*illustrated on preceding page*).

serves 6

for the pastry
1³/₄ cups/200g all-purpose flour · ¹/₄ tsp salt · ³/₄ stick + 1 tbsp/100g chilled unsalted butter, cubed · 2 egg yolks, beaten · 2 tbsp ice water · pinch saffron strands

for the filling
¹/₄ stick/25g butter · 2 large onions, chopped · 1 red bell pepper, seeded and chopped
1 green bell pepper, seeded and chopped · 1 small hot red chili, seeded and finely chopped
1 clove garlic, finely chopped · small bunch flat-leaf parsley, chopped · 10oz/300g chorizo
sausage, diced · ¹/₂lb/250g lean pork loin, finely diced · 3oz/90g Serrano ham
salt and ground black pepper

For the pastry, place the flour and salt in a bowl and add the cubes of cold butter. Gently and swiftly rub the fat into the flour, using your fingertips, until it resembles coarse breadcrumbs. Make a well in the center with your fist. Mix the egg yolks with the ice water and saffron strands. Reserving a little for glazing the pie, gradually add the egg mixture to the dry ingredients, a little at a time, using a knife to mix the dough as you go. Turn out the dough on to a floured surface and knead lightly until smooth. Shape into a ball, wrap in plastic wrap and leave to rest in the refrigerator until you have prepared the filling.

Heat the butter in a large skillet and cook the onions gently for about 10 minutes until softened. Add the red and green bell peppers, chili, and garlic and cook for a further 15 minutes until softened. Stir in the chopped parsley and season with a little salt and pepper to taste.

Preheat the oven to 350°F.

Roll out two-thirds of the pastry on a lightly floured surface to fit a 9in/23cm pie plate.

Mix the chorizo and pork into the pepper mixture and spoon into the pie shell. Lay the slices of Serrano ham on top. Brush the edges of the pastry with beaten egg mixture.

Roll out the remaining pastry to make a lid and lay it on top of the pie. Trim off any excess and crimp the edges between your finger and index finger. Make 3 small slashes in the top to release the steam. Brush the top with the remaining egg and saffron mixture and bak e in the oven for 50 minutes until golden. Leave to stand for a good 30 minutes to let everything settle before serving it in wedges.

vegetable and rice picnic pie

This was a pie my mother used to make regularly for snacks, school lunchboxes or for picnics. Rice cakes, or *torta* as they are known in Italy, are found with a multitude of flavorings, including ham, cheese, herbs, and vegetables. The uncooked rice cooks perfectly inside the pastry crust, giving a tasty, creamy filling that is sturdy enough to travel and to eat on the go.

serves 4–6

for the pastry
10oz/300g all purpose flour · pinch salt · $^2/_3$ cup/150ml water · 1 tsp olive oil · 2 tbsp milk, to glaze
beaten egg, to glaze

for the filling
1lb/500g spinach · 3 cups/300g thinly sliced zucchini · 1 onion, thinly sliced
$^1/_2$ cup/100g risotto rice · $^1/_2$ cup/50g grated Parmesan cheese · 2 eggs, beaten
1 tsp sea salt · salt and ground black pepper

To make the pastry, put the flour and salt in a bowl, then stir in the water and oil to make a smooth, firm dough. Cover with a damp cloth and leave to rest for at least 10 minutes.

Preheat the oven to 350°F.

Wash the spinach well and place in a large saucepan with just the water that clings to its leaves. Cook for 5 minutes until wilted completely. Leave to cool, then squeeze out any excess water and chop roughly.

In a large bowl, mix the spinach, zucchini, onion, rice, Parmesan, eggs, and a little salt and pepper.

Halve the pastry and roll out each piece until it is $^1/_4$in/5mm thick. Use one half to line an oiled 8 x 12in/20 x 30cm jelly roll pan. Spoon in the filling, then cover with the remaining pastry. Trim the edges and press well together to seal. To glaze, mix the milk and beaten egg and brush this on the pie lid, then sprinkle with salt. Bake for 40 minutes until golden brown. Serve warm or cold, cut into squares.

stargazy pie

This very famous pie from Cornwall in south-west England was originally made using pilchards and herrings. The fish were usually arranged so that their heads peeped out of a hole in the center of the pastry and they appeared to be gazing skyward. Although very dramatic, it is not the most practical of pies for eating. My version here uses fillets of mackerel, which still makes for a very tasty pie without changing the original ingredients combination too much *(illustrated on preceding pages)*.

serves 4

for the pastry
10oz/300g shortcrust pastry (see page 15) · beaten egg, to glaze

for the filling
1 tbsp/15g butter · 1 cup/50g breadcrumbs · 2 large potatoes, peeled, parboiled, and thinly sliced
2 strips bacon, chopped · 2 tbsp chopped chives · 2 tbsp chopped flat-leaf parsley · 4 fillets of
mackerel · 3 eggs, beaten · 2/3 cup/150ml heavy cream · salt and ground black pepper

Preheat the oven to 400°F.

Butter a 9in/23cm deep pie dish and sprinkle with breadcrumbs so that they stick to the sides. Arrange the potatoes in the base of the dish and sprinkle with half of the bacon and half of the chives and parsley. Season with a little salt and ground black pepper.

Lay the mackerel fillets on top and sprinkle with the remaining bacon, chives, parsley, and seasoning. Beat the eggs together with the cream and pour this over the fish.

Roll out the pastry to a thickness of about 1/8in/3mm. Cut a 3/4in/2cm strip from the rolled-out pastry. Brush the rim of the pie dish with water and place the pastry strip around the rim, pressing it down. Cut out a lid from the remaining pastry about 1in/2.5cm larger than the dish. Arrange a pie funnel in the center of the pie and place the pastry lid on top, pressing down to seal the edges. Trim off any excess pastry and crimp the edges with a fork, or between your thumb and index finger. Brush the top with beaten egg and bake for 10 minutes, then reduce the temperature to 350°F and bake for a further 20 minutes until the crust is crisp and golden and the filling is set. Serve hot with boiled new potatoes tossed in chopped fresh parsley.

freeform cheese, bacon, and onion pie

This is a great throw-it-together pie. You don't need any special pan or pie dish and most of the ingredients are pretty much store-cupboard staples. So simple, but the most delicious thing served with a crisp salad and a sharp lemon dressing.

serves 4

for the pastry
1lb/500g ready-made puff pastry · beaten egg, to glaze

for the filling
2 large mealy potatoes · 1 tbsp vegetable oil · 4 smoked bacon strips, cut into 3/4in/2cm pieces
2 large onions, thinly sliced · 1 3/4 cups/200g coarsely grated mature Cheddar cheese
3 tbsp heavy cream · ground black pepper

Preheat the oven to 400°F.

Place the potatoes in a saucepan and cover with cold water. Bring to a boil and cook for 10–15 minutes until the potatoes are tender. Drain and, when cool enough to handle, cut the potatoes into thin slices. Heat the oil in a large skillet and cook the bacon, stirring occasionally, for 2 minutes until beginning to color. Add the onions and cook for 4–5 minutes until softened but not colored. Set aside to cool.

Divide the pastry into two portions. Roll out one half to form a 10in/25cm square. Lay the pastry square on a lightly greased baking sheet and brush the edges lightly with beaten egg. Spread the sliced potatoes over the pastry, then top with the bacon and onions, leaving a 1in/2.5cm border all the way around. Sprinkle with the grated cheese and season with ground black pepper. Drizzle over the cream.

Roll out the second piece of pastry to form an 11in/28cm square. Place over the filling and press the edges together to join. Trim away any excess and cut a cross in the middle of the pie. Brush lightly with beaten egg and bake in the top of the oven for 10 minutes, then reduce the heat to 350°F and cook for a further 25–30 minutes, or until golden and risen.

Serve cut into wedges.

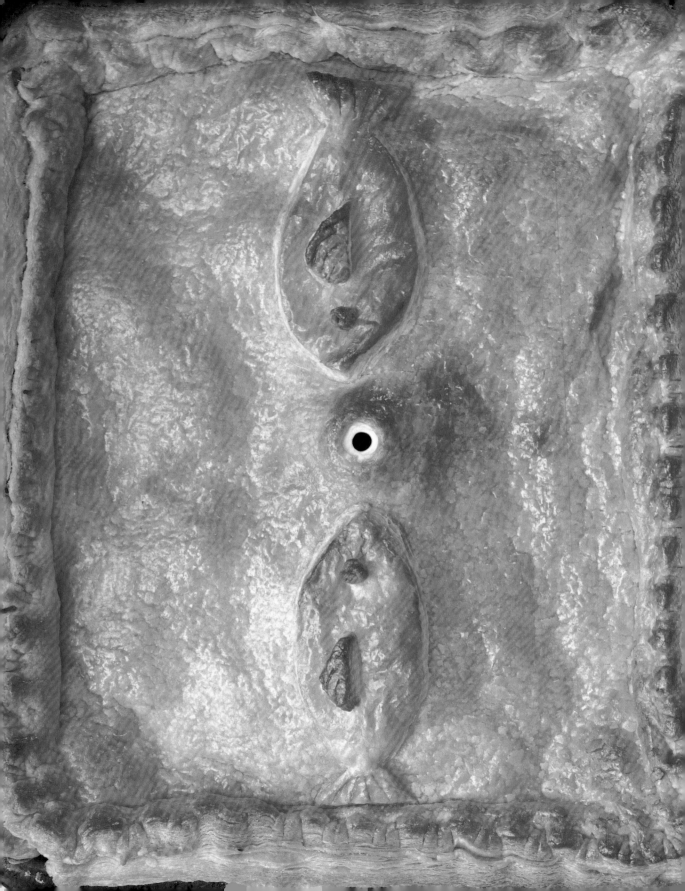

smoked fish and cider pie

A pie book would not be complete without a fish pie. I chose this classic as it's simple and delicious but has a wonderful flavor from the mixture of smoked fish and cider.

serves 4

for the pastry
12oz/350g ready-rolled puff pastry · beaten egg, to glaze

for the filling
1lb/450g fresh haddock fillet, skinned · 4oz/125g smoked haddock (finnan haddie) fillet, skinned
1 large potato, peeled, parboiled, and finely sliced · 3 tbsp/40g butter · 1 onion, finely chopped
$^1/_2$ cup/50g all-purpose flour · 1 $^3/_4$ cups/400ml strong cider · 3 tbsp crème fraîche or sour cream
$^3/_4$ cup/75g frozen peas · 2 tbsp chopped fresh parsley · 8oz/250g medium raw shrimp
salt and ground black pepper

Preheat the oven to 400°F.

Cut all the haddock into 1in/2.5cm pieces. Lay the potato slices in the base of a 6 cup/1.5 litre pie dish. Heat the butter in a medium saucepan until melted and foaming. Add the onion and cook for 5 minutes until soft. Add the flour and cook for a few minutes until it forms a smooth paste. Gradually pour in the cider, stirring constantly with a wooden spoon until you have a smooth thickened sauce. Remove from the heat and stir in the crème fraîche. Season with a little salt and plenty of ground black pepper. Stir in the peas, parsley, shrimp, and haddock pieces. Spoon the mixture into the pie dish on top of the potato.

Moisten the edges of the dish with a little water and place a pie funnel in the center of the filling. Unroll the pastry and lay it on top. Brush with the egg and bake for 35–40 minutes until golden.

cheshire cheese and onion pie

I have crossed English counties by mixing flavorsome red Leicester cheese in the pastry of this pie with creamy Cheshire cheese in the filling. It really works to give a moreish, delicious pie which is simplicity itself. The sliced potatoes cook in the steam generated inside the pie (saving you the job of precooking them), so don't be tempted to put a steam hole in the pastry.

serves 4

for the pastry
10oz/300g cheese pastry (see page 17), made with red Leicester cheese · 2 tbsp milk, to glaze

for the filling
1 bunch scallions, roughly chopped · 1 cup/125g crumbled Cheshire cheese · 4 tbsp crème fraîche or sour cream · 1 bunch chives, snipped · 1lb/500g mealy potatoes, peeled and very thinly sliced · salt and ground black pepper

Preheat the oven to 350°F.

Roll out about 6oz/175g of the pastry on a lightly floured surface and line a 9in/23cm shallow pie plate. Mix together the scallions, Cheshire cheese, crème fraîche, and snipped chives in a small bowl, seasoning with a little salt and plenty of ground black pepper.

Arrange the potatoes in layers with a few tablespoons of the scallions and cheese mixture spread between each layer. Continue until all the potatoes and cheese mixture are used up. Brush the edge of the pastry with a little milk.

Roll out the remaining pastry about 3/4in/2cm larger than the dish and then lay this over the top of the pie. Crimp the edges to seal and brush with a little milk to glaze, then bake for approximately 30 minutes.

Reduce the temperature to 325°F and cook for a further 40 minutes until the pastry is golden and the potatoes are cooked through. To test if the potatoes are cooked, simply insert a toothpick into the pie and test for tenderness.

If the pastry is cooking too quickly, place a loose piece of foil over the top.

Leave to cool slightly before serving so that the filling melds together perfectly. This will make it easier to slice and to serve in wedges.

fidget pie

This is a lovely old-fashioned recipe from Shropshire, England, traditionally served to the workers during harvest time. The name of this pie is said to have come from the fact that it was originally "fitched" or five-sided in shape. I just love the name of it and the combination of ingredients in the filling. Apples and bacon are perfect partners.

serves 4

for the pastry
10oz/300g shortcrust pastry (see page 15) · milk or beaten egg, to glaze

for the filling
3 tbsp/40g butter · 3 medium potatoes, peeled and finely sliced · 2 onions, sliced
2 cooking apples, peeled, cored, and sliced (weighing about ³/₄lb/350g prepared weight)
2 tsp finely chopped sage · 2 tsp light brown sugar · 3 slices sweetcure bacon, rind removed
and cut into ¹/₂in/1cm strips ²/₃ cup/150ml vegetable stock · salt and ground black pepper

Preheat the oven to 350°F.

Heat the butter in a large skillet and gently cook the potatoes, onions, and apples in the butter until just golden. Stir in the sage. Transfer the potatoes, onions and apples to a 4 cup/1 litre pie dish, sprinkle on the sugar and season with salt and pepper.

Place the bacon in the skillet and cook lightly in the remaining fat until golden, then add to the pie dish. Pour over the stock.

On a lightly floured surface, roll out the pastry to a thickness of about ¹/₈in/3mm and cover the pie, trimming the edges. Make a steam hole and decorate with the trimmings. Brush with milk or egg.

Bake for 30 minutes, then reduce the heat to 325°F for a further 10–15 minutes until the pie is golden brown.

cornmeal crust chili pie

The crusty cornmeal pastry of this pie soaks up the juices from the chili and also helps to concentrate the flavors of the filling during baking.

serves 4–6

for the pastry
300g/10oz shortcrust pastry (see page 15), $^1/_2$ cup/50g of the flour replaced with coarse yellow cornmeal or polenta · beaten egg, to glaze

for the filling
2 tbsp sunflower oil · I large onion, finely chopped · 2 cloves garlic, finely chopped
I tsp ground cumin · I tsp smoked paprika · 1lb/450g ground beef · I red bell pepper,
seeded and diced · 2 green chilies, chopped · 14oz/400g can chopped tomatoes
14oz/400g can chili beans · salt and ground black pepper

Heat the oil in a large saucepan. Add the onion and garlic and cook for 5 minutes or until softened but not colored. Add the cumin, paprika, ground beef, red bell pepper, and chilies and cook for a further 5 minutes until lightly browned, breaking up any lumps of beef with a wooden spoon. Pour in the tomatoes and chili beans, then season to taste. Bring to a boil, reduce the heat and simmer gently for 30 minutes or until the beef is tender and the sauce has slightly reduced. Spoon the mixture into a 6 cup/1.5 litre pie dish and leave to cool.

Preheat the oven to 400°F.

Roll out the pastry to a thickness of about $^1/_8$in/3mm. Cut a $^3/_4$in/2cm strip from the rolled-out pastry. Brush the rim of the pie dish with water and place the pastry strip around the rim, pressing it down. Cut out a lid from the remaining pastry about 1in/2.5cm larger than the dish.

Sit a pie funnel into the center of the filling to support the pastry and stop it from sinking into the filling and becoming soggy. Place the pastry lid over the top of the dish and press down on the edges to seal. Trim off any excess pastry and crimp the edges with a fork, or between your thumb and index finger. Brush with beaten egg and make a hole in the center to reveal the pie funnel. Use the pastry trimmings to make decorations for the surface of the pie. Bake for 30–35 minutes until the crust is crisp and golden.

ham, leek, and cider pan pie

This idea was taken from a traditional Lancashire pie recipe which ingeniously puts a light suet pastry lid on the pie filling while it is still in the pan and the whole pie is then cook ed on the hob. The creamy ham and leek filling really works well with the tender pastry crust which soaks up all the juices. This method not only produces a pie that tastes fantastic and is easy to make but also saves on the all-important washing up.

serves 4

for the pastry
I cup/100g all-purpose flour · 2oz/50g vegetable suet, grated · pinch salt · 1/4 tsp baking powder

for the filling
1/4 stick/25g butter · 2 large leeks, chopped · I 3/4lb/900g unsmoked ham joint, cut into
Iin/2.5cm cubes · 2 carrots, peeled and roughly chopped · 3 celery stalks, finely sliced
I large potato, peeled and chopped · handful fresh thyme leaves · 2 tbsp all-purpose flour
I 3/4 cups/400ml strong cider · 3 tbsp crème fraîche or sour cream · salt and ground
black pepper

Heat the butter in a large flameproof casserole and gently cook the leeks for a few minutes until beginning to soften. Add the cubed ham, all the vegetables, and the thyme and toss together well with the flour. Increase the heat, pour in the cider, and bring to a boil. Reduce to a gentle simmer and stir through the crème fraîche. Season with a little salt and ground b lack pepper and simmer for 35 minutes until the meat is tender and the sauce thick ened.

Meanwhile make the pastry by combining the flour, suet, salt, and baking powder in a large bowl and mixing to a dough with about 2–3 tab lespoons of water. On a lightly floured surface, roll out the pastry to 1/2in/I cm thick and lay it over the stew in the dish. Cover with a lid and simmer for 30 minutes until the pastry is puffed up and cooked through.

If you want to brown the top of the pastry to create a golden cr ust before serving, simply place the dish under a preheated broiler for 3–4 minutes.

handpie

Small savory pies really are little treasure chests of pure delight. They always look so perfect and enticing and make you just want to take a bite to reveal the secret of what lies within.

Cold hand-held pies are ideal for picnics and encasing them in crisp shortcrust pastry will make them sturdy enough to withstand a journey. Hot individual pies, served straight from the oven with tender, juicy meat and vegetable fillings, make the best small pies for dinner, served with mash and peas. Alternatively, you can use them as little savory bites, served as an appetizer with drinks.

However you decide to enjoy them, the following recipes will suit any occasion and can be eaten without the aid of a plate—just hold your pie aloft and eat!

chicken and mushroom pies

These individual chicken and mushroom pies are made extra special by adding dried wild mushrooms and a splash of sherry and cream. Far grander than store-bought versions, they are indulgent little pies that will certainly impress your friends. As you're already pulling out all the stops, experiment with some creative pastry decoration too.

makes 6 pies

for the pastry
13oz/400g rich shortcrust pastry (see page 16) · beaten egg, to glaze

for the filling
³/₄oz/20g dried wild mushrooms · ¹/₄ stick/25g butter · 1 tbsp olive oil · 1 large onion,
finely chopped · 2 cloves garlic, chopped · 2 chicken thighs, skinned and cut into pieces about
³/₄in/1.5cm square · 2 large chicken breasts, cut into pieces about ³/₄in/1.5cm square
8oz/250g cremini mushrooms, sliced · 3 tbsp dry sherry or Marsala · 3¹/₂ tbsp all-purpose
flour · 2 tbsp heavy cream · small bunch flat-leaf parsley, roughly chopped

Place the dried mushrooms in a small bowl and cover with boiling water. Leave to soak for about
20 minutes. Drain the dried mushrooms, reserving ³/₄ cup/200ml of the soaking liquid. Strain the
reserved soaking liquid through a fine sieve to remove any gritty bits. Chop the mushrooms finely.

Meanwhile, heat the butter and oil in a large skillet and gently cook the onion for about 5 minutes
until softened and golden. Stir in the garlic, chicken, and chestnut mushrooms and cook on a high
heat for a further 6 minutes. Add the sherry or Marsala and simmer rapidly for a minute.

Reduce the temperature to medium and stir in the flour until evenly mixed in. Add the drained dried
mushrooms and reserved soaking liquid. Simmer together for about 5 minutes, then add the cream
and cook for a further 5 minutes until the sauce is thickened. Stir in the parsley and season well to
taste. Set aside to cool.

Preheat the oven to 350°F.

Roll out the pastry and cut out 6 x 6in/15cm disks to line
6 x 4in/10cm small individual pie pans. Press the pastry into
the bottom and up the sides of each pan, allowing a little
overhang. Fill each shell with the cooled filling and either cut out
6 x 4in/10cm disks from the remaining pastry for lids or cut into
thick strips to make a lattice pastry top. Brush the tops with
beaten egg and bake for 30–35 minutes until golden. Leave the
pies in the pans to cool for about 5 minutes before removing.
Serve immediately.

mini pork and pancetta pies

These are the ultimate picnic pies—sturdy enough to withstand a journey and tasty enough to be devoured when you arrive, or maybe even on the way. They can be made up to 1 day ahead and are also a great choice for packed lunches, served with crunchy radishes and scallions.

makes 12 pies

for the pastry
10oz/300g shortcrust pastry (see page 15) · beaten egg, to glaze

for the filling
1 bunch scallions, finely chopped · pinch chili flakes · 1/2lb/225g pork loin, finely chopped with a knife or in a food processor · 4oz/100g pancetta, finely chopped · small bunch chives, snipped small bunch parsley, finely chopped · salt and ground black pepper · 12 quail's eggs, soft-cooked and peeled

Preheat the oven to 400°F.

For the filling, mix together all the ingredients except the quail's eggs in a large bowl, seasoning well to taste.

Roll out the pastry on a lightly floured surface and cut out 12 x 4in/9cm disks to fit a 12-hole muffin pan and 12 x 3in/7cm disks for the lids. Carefully press the larger disks into the holes of the muffin pan. Half fill each with the pork filling, top with a soft-cooked quail's egg, then add another layer of filling.

Brush the edges of each pie with a little egg and then place a lid on top, pressing the edges together to seal. Make a hole in the top of each pie, brush the tops with egg to glaze and bake for 20 minutes. Reduce the oven temperature to 325°F and bake for a further 25–30 minutes until the pastry is golden and the filling is cooked through. Leave to cool in the pan for 5 minutes before transferring to a wire rack to cool completely.

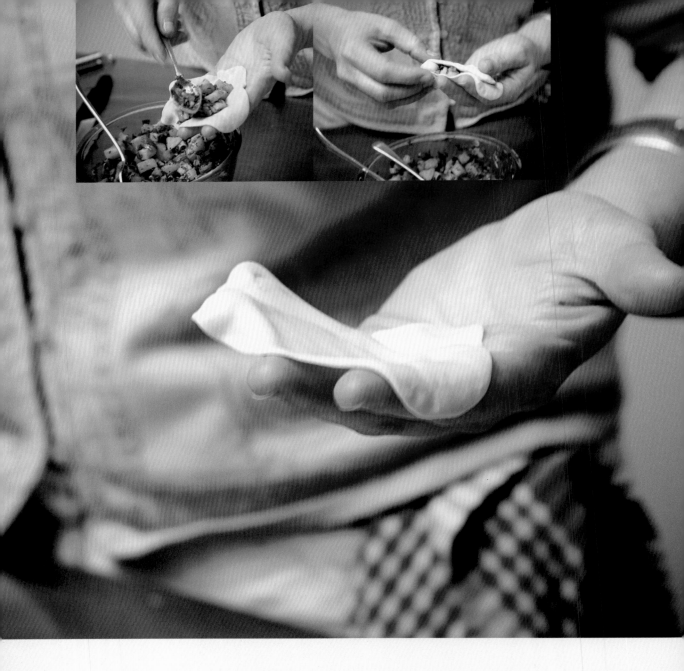

masala pasties

These tasty, spiced pasties were inspired by South Indian masala dosa pancakes, which have a potato, green chili, and onion filling. They are delicious served with a dipping sauce made from mango chutney, chopped cilantro, and lemon juice *(illustrated on preceding pages)*.

makes approximately 20

for the pastry
2 cups/225g all-purpose flour · ½ tsp salt · 2 tbsp vegetable oil

for the filling
1¼lb/600g potatoes, peeled and cut into ¾in/1.5cm dice · 2 tbsp olive oil · ½ tsp cumin seeds
½ tsp black mustard seeds · ½ tsp garam masala · 1 green chili, seeded and finely chopped
2 cloves garlic, finely chopped · 6 scallions, finely chopped · juice of ½ lemon · small bunch
cilantro, chopped · vegetable oil, for deep-frying

To make the pastry, place the flour and salt in a large mixing bowl. Add the oil and mix together, using your fingertips to rub it in. Once the oil and flour are combined, gradually mix in about 1 cup/250ml of water, a little at a time, until you have a firm dough. Knead the dough for 5–7 minutes, until smooth. Form into a ball, brush with a little oil, and set aside covered with either a damp cloth or plastic wrap while you prepare the filling.

Place the potatoes in a saucepan and cover with water. Bring to a boil and simmer for 12–15 minutes until just tender but still holding their shape. Drain well.

Heat the olive oil in a large skillet and gently heat the cumin seeds and mustard seeds until they begin to pop, then stir in the garam masala. Add the drained potatoes to the pan and cook gently in the spices and oil until coated in the mixture and beginning to brown—this should take only about 5–8 minutes. Mix in the chili and garlic and cook for a further 2 minutes. Remove from the heat and stir in the scallions, lemon juice, and chopped cilantro. Set aside and allow to cool.

Divide the dough into 20 balls. Flatten each ball and roll out on a floured surface to make a circle approximately 4in/10cm across. Spoon a heaped tablespoon of the potato mixture into the center of each disk, then brush the edge with a little water. Fold over the pastry to form a semicircle and seal by pressing the edges together. Continue in this way until you have made 20 pasties, covering the finished pasties with a damp cloth or plastic wrap as you make the rest.

Heat about 4in/9cm of oil in a wok or heavy-based saucepan over a medium heat. To test the temperature, drop a little of the pastry into the oil—it should sizzle immediately. Fry the pasties in batches for 2–3 minutes until lightly browned. Remove with a slotted spoon and drain on paper towels. Serve warm with a mango chutney and cilantro dipping sauce.

cornish pasties

Originating from the county of Cornwall in southwest England, this traditional workman's midday meal used to be marked with his initials—be he a miner, fisherman, or farmer. The fillings varied—no doubt depending on what was available, and the housekeeping finances. They were usually made with meat and potatoes, although other vegetables were added, in season. Cornish pasties are still one of the most popular handheld pies and when made well are a delicious combination of a simple, nourishing filling and the lightest crust ever. Place the shortening and butter in the freezer for about 20 minutes before you start to make the pasties as this will give you a really crisp crust.

makes 4 large pasties

for the pastry
3¹/₂ cups/450g bread flour · pinch salt · 1 stick/100g lard, or ¹/₂ cup shortening, chilled in the freezer · 1 stick/100g butter, chilled in the freezer · beaten egg, to glaze

for the filling
¹/₂lb/250g beef skirt, chopped into rough cubes about ¹/₄in/5mm square · ¹/₂lb/250g potatoes, peeled and diced into ¹/₄in/5mm cubes · ¹/₂lb/250g rutabaga, peeled and diced into ¹/₄in/5mm cubes 1 onion, finely chopped · 1 tbsp vegetable oil · salt and ground black pepper

For the pastry, sift the flour and salt into a bowl, then grate in the lard, or shortening, and butter straight from the freezer. Gently mix into the flour and stir in just enough cold water to bring the mixture together to make a firm dough. Knead briefly and form into a smooth ball. Wrap in plastic wrap and chill in the refrigerator for 20 minutes.

Preheat the oven to 350°F.

For the filling, combine the beef with the potatoes, rutabaga, onion, vegetable oil, a little salt, and black pepper.

Cut the dough ball into quarters and roll out each quarter into an 8in/20cm disk. Divide the beef and vegetable mixture between the 4 pastry disks, piling it along the middle of the pastry. Brush the rim of the pastry with beaten egg. Bring up the pastry from either side to meet in the middle and pinch together to make a scalloped edge down the center. Make 2 slits with the point of a sharp knife on each side so that steam can escape through the pastry during cooking.

Place on a baking sheet and brush with beaten egg. Bake for 35–40 minutes until the crust is golden. The pasties are delicious served hot, straight from the oven.

sausage rolls

It couldn't be simpler to make delicious sausage rolls—there are good sausages around as well as great ready-made puff pastry, but you can use ordinary sausagemeat as well. These are made using English sausages spruced up with onion, herbs, and a little Parmesan cheese for flavor. I love no-nonsense, substantial sausage rolls—big and juicy ones that you can sink your teeth into—but for a more refined affair you can make little bite-sized ones to serve with drinks.

makes 8 large or 16 small rolls

for the pastry
1lb/500g ready-made puff pastry · beaten egg, to glaze

for the filling
8 large English sausages, skins removed, or 1½lb/750g sausagemeat · 1 small onion, finely chopped · 3–4 sage leaves, finely chopped · 3 tbsp chopped flat-leaf parsley · 3 tbsp grated Parmesan cheese salt and ground black pepper

Preheat the oven to 400°F.

To make the filling, mix the sausage meat in a bowl with the onion, sage, parsley, and Parmesan. It's easiest to mulch it all together with your hands. Season with salt and ground black pepper.

Now assemble the first batch of sausage rolls. Cut the dough in half and roll out one piece to make a long oblong shape, 16 × 6½in/40 × 17cm and ⅛in/3mm thick. Form half the filling into a long log-shape which will run the whole length of the pastry. Place the sausage log ¼in/5mm in from the edge of the pastry. Egg-wash the entire length of the pastry strip, then fold the pastry over the log and press down well to seal the edges, either crimping them with your fingers or pressing down with a fork.

Cut the log into 4 individual rolls if you want large ones, or 8 bite-sized rolls. Brush with egg to glaze and then place on a baking sheet lined with greased baking parchment, leaving plenty of space in between each one. Place the sheet in the oven for 35–40 minutes and bake until the rolls are golden, risen, and flaky. Remove from the oven and allow to cool slightly on a wire rack.

While the sausage rolls are baking, prepare a second batch using the remaining pastry and filling. Serve the rolls while still warm.

Homemade sausage rolls straight from the oven have got to be the best handheld pies ever—well my dog and I think so anyway.

smoked salmon, shrimp, and herb pies

Crammed with smoked salmon, shrimp, and herbs, these pies are a luxurious treat. Short-cut flaky pastry provides the perfect contrast to the tasty filling, giving a crisp, light, and buttery coating. These pies are great served hot or cold with a crisp green salad, or wrap them up and take them to the shore for a picnic. Fish eaten by the sea always tastes fantastic.

makes 6 pies

for the pastry
15oz/450g short-cut flaky pastry (see page 19) · beaten egg, to glaze

for the filling
1/2lb/250g smoked salmon, chopped · 1/2lb/250g small raw shrimp · 1/4 cup/25g grated Parmesan cheese · 2 tbsp chopped fresh dill · I clove garlic, finely chopped
generous 1/2 cup mascarpone cheese · grated zest of I lemon · ground black pepper

Preheat the oven to 400°F.

On a floured surface, roll out the pastry to form a large sheet 1/8in/3mm thick and cut out 6 disks 5in/12cm in diameter and 6 disks 6in/15cm in diameter.

Mix together the smoked salmon, shrimp, Parmesan, chopped dill, garlic, mascarpone, lemon zest, and plenty of ground black pepper.

Dollop 2–3 tablespoons of the mixture in the center of each of the smaller disks. Brush the edges of the disks with a little beaten egg.

Position the larger disks on top and press the pastry edges together to seal. Use a sharp knife to create a small hole in the center of each pie and then transfer to a baking sheet. Brush the pies with a little beaten egg and bake for about 20 minutes until golden and crisp.

Serve hot or cold.

fennel and gruyère puffs

These little pies are really simple to make using good-quality, ready-made puff pastry. Don't worry if they look like strange UFOs when they come out of the oven—they will still taste delicious and are great served warm as appetizers with drinks.

makes 12 puffs

for the pastry
12oz/350g ready-rolled puff pastry · beaten egg, to glaze

for the filling
2 tbsp olive oil · 1/4 stick/25g butter · 1 small onion, finely chopped · 1 small fennel bulb, finely chopped · 1 tsp fennel seeds · 3/4 cup/75g grated Gruyère cheese
salt and ground black pepper

For the filling, heat the oil and butter in a large skillet and add the onion, fennel, and fennel seeds and fry very gently for about 15 minutes until softened, then stir through the grated cheese. Remove from the heat and allow to cool slightly.

Unroll the pastry and cut out 12 disks 2in/5cm in diameter for the lids and 12 disks 1 1/2in/4cm in diameter for the bases. Place the smaller pastry bases on a large baking sheet and brush the edges with beaten egg.

Spoon the cooled fennel mixture onto the pastry bases, leaving a 1/2in/1cm margin. Position the pastry lids on top and use a fork to press the pastry edges together to seal. Chill in the refrigerator for 30 minutes.

Preheat the oven to 425°F.

Brush the top of the puffs with beaten egg and bake for 20 minutes until golden brown and puffed up. Serve warm.

lamb en croûtes

These little parcels comprise tasty layers of spinach, mushrooms, and tender lamb, all wrapped in rich shortcrust pastry which seals in the juices and keeps everything deliciously moist.

makes 4 *en croûtes*

for the pastry
10oz/300g rich shortcrust pastry (see page 16) · beaten egg, to glaze

for the filling
4 tbsp olive oil · 4 lamb fillets, or slices from the leg, each weighing about 5oz/150g
large knob butter · 4oz/125g cremini mushrooms, finely chopped · 1 clove garlic, finely
chopped · 4 sun-dried tomatoes, finely chopped · 2 canned anchovy fillets, finely chopped
small bunch fresh mint finely chopped · 7oz/200g large spinach leaves · 3 tbsp Marsala
1 tbsp redcurrant jelly · 1$^{1}/_{4}$ cups/300ml lamb stock · salt and ground black pepper

Preheat the oven to 400°F.

For the filling, heat half the oil in a large skillet and seal the lamb until browned. Remove from the skillet and set aside. In the same skillet heat the remaining oil with the butter until the butter is foaming. Stir in the mushrooms and cook for about 15 minutes until browned and tender. Stir in the garlic, sun-dried tomatoes, and anchovies and season to taste. Cook for 5 minutes until the mixture has a soft, paste-like consistency. Remove from the heat, stir in the chopped mint and set aside.

Wash the spinach leaves and place in a saucepan with just the water that clings to them. Cook gently, being careful not to break the leaves, until just wilted. Drain well and leave to cool. Spread the mushroom paste over each piece of lamb and carefully wrap the spinach leaves around the paste.

Roll out the pastry on a lightly floured surface until about $^{1}/_{8}$in/3mm thick. Cut into 4 and wrap each piece around a piece of lamb. Place the parcels, sealed side down, on a baking sheet and brush with beaten egg. Bake for 25–30 minutes until the crust is crispy and golden.

Meanwhile, reheat the skillet used for the lamb and pour in the Marsala. Deglaze the skillet, scraping up any bits left on the bottom, then stir in the redcurrant jelly. Add the stock and simmer gently until the mixture is syrupy and has reduced by about half. Serve the *en croûtes* with the Marsala gravy.

asparagus turnovers

These are sort of half-pie and half-tart—a delicious, creamy ham and cheese filling with asparagus spears wrapped in puff pastry. Very simple and very tasty, they are perfect for a quick supper *(illustrated on preceding pages)*.

makes 6 turnovers

for the pastry
1lb/500g ready-made puff pastry

for the filling
1/2 cup/100g cream cheese · grated zest and juice 1/2 lemon · 1/2oz/15g fresh chives, chopped · 1/4 cup/25g grated Parmesan cheese · 6 thin slices cooked smoked ham · 1 1/4lb/600g asparagus spears, trimmed · 1 tbsp olive oil · salt and ground black pepper

Preheat the oven to 400°F.

Roll out the pastry on a lightly floured surface to form a sheet 1/8in/3mm thick. Now cut it into 6 even-sized squares.

Place the cream cheese, lemon zest and juice, chives, and most of the Parmesan in a bowl and mix together well. Season with a little salt and ground black pepper. Divide the mixture between the 6 pastry squares, spreading it out a little, then lay a slice of cooked ham on the cheese. Place a few asparagus spears diagonally on top of the ham. Now fold the bottom corner of each pastry square over the base of the spears, leaving the tips exposed. Brush the edges of the pastry with a little water. Fold over each side of the pastry to form a pouch, pressing down gently to seal.

Brush the top of the pastry and asparagus tips with the oil and sprinkle with the remaining Parmesan. Bake for 20 minutes until the pastry is golden and puffed and the asparagus spears are tender. Serve immediately.

goat's cheese, roasted garlic, and sweet potato parcels

Oozing goat's cheese wrapped in flaky pastry with the sweetness of roasted garlic and sweet potatoes—what a joy! These parcels make a divine supper served with a salad of peppery Belgian endive and arugula leaves.·

makes 4 parcels

for the pastry
12oz/350g ready-rolled puff pastry · beaten egg, to glaze

for the filling
1 tbsp olive oil · 2 sweet potatoes, total weight about 1lb/500g, peeled and thinly sliced
3 sprigs fresh thyme · 8 cloves garlic, skins left on · 2 soft barrel-shaped goat's cheeses
salt and ground black pepper

Preheat the oven to 400°F.

Toss the olive oil, sweet potatoes, most of the thyme, and the garlic in a large roasting pan. Add a little salt and plenty of ground black pepper and roast on a high shelf in the oven for about 15 minutes until the sweet potatoes are tender and golden and the garlic is soft and paste-like when squeezed. Remove from the roasting pan and leave to cool.

Unroll the pastry and cut it into 4 squares of about 7in/18cm.

Squeeze the roasted garlic out of its skin and spread over the base of each pastry square, using about 2 cloves of garlic per square. Use half of the sweet potato slices to cover the garlic, and add a little more thyme. Cut each goat's cheese in half and arrange on top of the sweet potatoes. Arrange the remaining sweet potato slices on top.

Fold the corners of each pastry square into the center to make an envelope and cover the filling. Crimp the edges to seal. Place the parcels on a baking sheet, brush with beaten egg and bake for 20 minutes until the crust is golden and puffed and the cheese has softened. Eat while the cheese is still warm.

empanadillas

These small, crescent-shaped pasties are traditionally served as tapas with drinks but are equally good eaten at any time. The filling reflects both North African and Catalan influences with the use of cumin, paprika, and the sweet contrast of raisins. The dough has a soft, pliable texture, making it easy to shape and form the little pasties.

makes 20 empanadillas

for the pastry
12oz/350g all-purpose plain flour · ¼ tsp salt
1½ sticks/175g butter, melted · 1 egg, beaten
½ cup/100ml warm water · milk, to glaze

for the filling
1 tbsp vegetable oil · 1 onion, finely chopped
1½ cups/350g ground beef · 1 red bell pepper, finely chopped · 2 cloves garlic, finely chopped
1 tbsp tomato paste . 1 tsp chili flakes · 1 tsp cumin seeds · 1 tsp smoked paprika
¼ cup/25g raisins · salt and ground black pepper

To make the pastry, sift the flour and salt into a large bowl. Stir in the butter and egg and then gradually work in enough of the warm water to make a firm dough. Knead for 5–10 minutes until the dough is smooth. Leave to rest, covered in plastic wrap, for 15 minutes while you prepare the filling.

For the filling, heat the oil in a large pan and cook the onion for a few minutes until it begins to soften. Stir in the ground beef and cook until browned. Add the rest of the ingredients and season well with salt and plenty of ground black pepper. Add a few tablespoons of water at this stage if the mixture looks too dry. Simmer for 5 minutes and then remove from the heat and leave to cool.

Preheat the oven to 400°F.

Roll out the pastry to a thickness of about ⅛in/3mm. Using a saucer as a template, cut out 24 disks about 5in/12cm in diameter. Divide the filling between the dough disks and moisten the edges with a little water. Fold the dough over to enclose the filling and press along the edges to seal. Pinch the sealed edges and twist over to create a rope effect, or simply press a fork along the edges. Glaze with a little milk and bake for 10–15 minutes until golden. Serve warm.

scallop, crab, and cayenne pies

It really makes sense to use the scallop shells as pie dishes for these tasty individual pies. Just give them a good scrub once you've removed the scallops. Alternatively, ask your fish supplier to keep some shells aside for you, as not all sell scallops in the shell.

makes 4 pies

for the pastry
12oz/350g ready-rolled puff pastry · milk, to glaze

for the filling
1¹/₂ tbsp butter · 2 shallots, finely chopped · 6 thin slices pancetta, finely chopped
8 large scallops, including the coral · 5oz/150g white crab meat · pinch cayenne pepper
grated zest of ¹/₂ lemon · 2 tbsp finely chopped flat-leaf parsley · 3 tbsp crème fraîche or
plain yogurt · salt and ground black pepper

Preheat the oven to 400°F.

Heat the butter in a small skillet and gently cook the shallots for a few minutes. Add the pancetta and cook for a further 3 minutes. Slice each scallop horizontally into 3 disks and halve the coral. Place the scallops, corals, and crab meat in a bowl and stir in the shallots and pancetta with the cayenne, lemon zest, and parsley. Stir through the crème fraîche or yogurt and season with salt and black pepper.

Divide the mixture between 4 cleaned and dried scallop shells and place on a baking sheet.

Roll out the pastry to a thickness of ¹/₈in/3mm and cut out 4 disks of pastry about ¹/₂in/1cm larger than the scallop shells. Lay each piece of pastry loosely over the top of each shell so that it covers the filling, press it down on to the shell edge to shape, then cut away any excess pastry. Brush with a little milk and bake for 15 minutes until the pastry is puffed and golden. Serve immediately.

scotch pies

Large numbers of Scotch pies are sold every day in Scotland—many at half-time during soccer matches. They are the ultimate hot fast food, easily eaten in the hand or served with gravy, peas, or beans. Traditionally they're made using straight-sided molds 3½in/8cm in diameter and about 1½in/4cm deep, but you could easily use an upturned jelly jar. The pastry lid is pressed on top of the pie slightly lower than the rim to create a space for the gravy.

Each butcher or baker has their own recipe with an individual mixture of spices and secret ingredients, but Scotch pies always contain lamb or mutton and a grinding of mace or nutmeg. Try to buy good-quality lean ground lamb as it really does make a difference to the finished pie.

If you don't want to bake all your pies at once, you can freeze them uncooked and simply defrost and bake when desired *(illustrated on preceding pages)*.

makes 8 pies

for the pastry
15oz/450g hot-water crust pastry (see page 21) · beaten egg, to glaze

for the filling
1 tsp vegetable oil · 2 cups/450g lean ground lamb · 1 tsp Worcestershire sauce
1 small onion, finely chopped · ¼ tsp ground nutmeg · 4 tbsp lamb stock
salt and ground black pepper

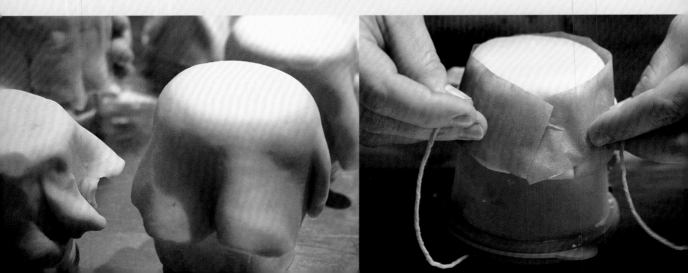

Preheat the oven to 350°F.

Use the oil to lightly grease the outer sides and bottoms of 8 jelly jars measuring 3½in/8cm in diameter (if you don't have 8 jars just make the pastry cases in 2 batches). Divide the pastry into 2 pieces. Place 1 in the refrigerator to make the lids and use the other to form 8 balls. On a lightly floured surface, roll out the balls to an even thickness of about ¼in/5mm, making pastry disks large enough to fit the upturned jelly jar bottoms and to come about 2½in/6cm down the sides of the jars. Press each disk onto the bottom of a jar and up against the sides, then set aside to cool.

Cut 8 strips of baking parchment or waxed paper the same depth as the pastry cases and long enough to wrap around the jars. Wrap each strip of paper around a case and secure with string. Place the finished pie shells in the refrigerator to firm up for about 30 minutes.

Meanwhile, mix all of the filling ingredients together, seasoning well with salt and ground black pepper.

Gently slide the pastry cases off the jars and place them on a baking sheet. Divide the meat mixture between the pastry cases, pressing it down well.

Roll out the remaining pastry to make 8 lids for the pies. Dampen the edges of the pies and place a lid on each, pressing them down lower than the rim. Crimp the edges with your fingers to seal.

Brush with beaten egg to glaze and cut a hole in the center, to allow steam to escape. Bake for 45 minutes, or until lightly golden, then serve hot with gravy (see page 185) poured on top and into the steam hole.

Barney's beef and stilton "corner-shop" pies

This is my great friend Barney's genius recipe for the most delicious and simple pies you'll ever taste. The "corner-shop" reference is where the genius bit comes in. No need for weighing or any tricky techniques, the pastry for these pies is pure simplicity and uses ready-weighed ingredients that are all available at your local corner shop, or neighborhood store.

This recipe makes enough filling for 8 individual pies or, like me, you can eat half the meat as a stew on the day you cook it and freeze or chill the other half as a pie filling. The filling is basically beef braised in red wine, given an extra kick by a splash of balsamic vinegar and a sprinkling of chili. The Stilton cheese, which is crumbled in just before the lids go on, gives the pies their sublime flavor.

makes 8 pies

for the pastry
1lb bag or 4 cups/500g all-purpose flour · 2 sticks/250g butter, diced · 1 egg, beaten
1/3 cup/70–100ml water · salt and ground black pepper

for the filling
2 tbsp sunflower oil · 2lb/1kg braising beef, cut into very large chunks · 4 carrots,
peeled and cut into very large chunks · 1 large onion, roughly chopped · 1 clove garlic
small pinch chili flakes · 4 tbsp all-purpose flour · big splash balsamic vinegar
1 bottle full-bodied red wine · 1 bouquet garni (tie a bunch of parsley stalks, a few
bay leaves, and a bunch of thyme together with string) · 1 1/4 cups/150g crumbled Stilton cheese

To make the pastry, tip the flour, butter, a pinch of salt, and some pepper into a food processor
and pulse until the mixture has the texture of breadcrumbs. Pour in the egg and water and pulse
again until the pastry comes together to form a ball. Wrap and chill in the refrigerator for at least
30 minutes before using.

Preheat the oven to 325°F.

Heat the oil in a large flameproof casserole until smoking, add half the beef and leave it to brown for
about 5 minutes (don't be tempted to prod it, stir it, or lift it up). Stir once and continue to brown the
meat, then remove it to a plate with a slotted spoon and repeat with the second batch of beef.

Once the second batch of beef has been removed, add the carrots, onion, garlic, and chili to the pan
and cook for 8–10 minutes until the vegetables are starting to soften. Stir in the flour and cook for
2 minutes until the flour begins to brown. Add a splash of balsamic vinegar and allow the mixture to
simmer for 2 minutes, then stir in the red wine. Tip the beef and any juices back into the pan and season
generously with salt and a little pepper. Bring to a boil, add the bouquet garni, cover and place in the
oven for about 2 hours until the meat is meltingly tender. Remove from the oven and leave to cool.

Turn the oven up to 425°F and heat a baking sheet while you roll out the pastry dough. Roll out
the dough on a floured surface to 1/8in/3mm thick and cut out pieces to fit 8 individual pie pans
(or foil molds).

Spoon the cooled filling into the pastry shells and sprinkle on the Stilton. Cut out the remaining
pastry to make lids for the pies. Wet the pastry edges with a little water and place the lids on top.
Seal the edges by pressing together, then trim away any excess pastry.

Place the pies on the hot sheet and bake for 10 minutes, then lower the oven temperature to
350°F and bake for 30 minutes until the tops are golden. Remove from the oven and leave to rest
for 10 minutes. The pies should now turn out of their pans easily and the bottoms should be crisp.

noblepie

These are not everyday pies, but something to create for a special occasion. They are "noble" because of the time and effort needed to create all the curves, flutings, cornices, roses, diamonds, circles, and leaves used for decoration. I guarantee a real sense of achievement when you remove the pie from its pan and present it to be sliced.

Steeped in history, these pies originate from the days when pastry was used simply as a container to protect and preserve the meat inside and was then discarded rather than eaten (though of course today we wouldn't dream of throwing it away). As a result, these pies use hot-water crust pastry (see page 21), which defies all the normal rules for pastry making and gives a pastry of considerable strength which is sturdy enough to act as a container.

Hot-water crust is a filling pastry because the pie walls must have thickness for strength and also to withstand the long cooking time needed to heat the dense filling inside. The pastry absorbs the rich meat juices and fat during cooking, but remains crisp outside.

Noble pies are often called "raised" pies because they are raised or shaped by hand and were traditionally prepared by pressing the dough on to the outside of a wooden mold. If you don't have a special pan or mold, you can form your pie around a jelly jar or in a cake pan with a removable base. Think of the dough as a piece of clay—it is warm and malleable and you can easily shape it into the mold or pan, repairing any cracks and holes.

The filling of a raised pie shrinks during cooking and the gap is filled with a savory jelly—hot stock which sets when cold. The jelly adds flavor and also keeps the meat moist. It's very simple to make, but does mean planning a couple of days ahead. For a good stock, use the bones from the meat you are using and simmer for a few hours with pig's feet, vegetables, and herbs. The stock will keep in the refrigerator for a few days until you need it.

raised game pie

This pie looks rather spectacular when cooked in a traditional pie mold. You can pick up molds of this sort from vintage cookware shops and even hunt them out on the web. They are rather expensive to buy new and an investment only if you know you are going to use them regularly. However, this pie is equally wonderful made in a loose-bottomed spring-form cake pan.

You can vary the filling depending on what you want to use and what is around at the time: venison, pheasant, and wild rabbit are all delicious. My butcher is a game specialist and so has game mix ready prepared, boned, and chopped, which makes life very easy.

serves 8

for the pastry
1lb/500g hot-water crust pastry (see page 21) to fill an 8in/20cm deep pie mold
beaten egg, to glaze

for the filling
1/4 stick/25g butter · 1 onion, finely chopped · 2 cloves garlic, finely chopped
1 3/4lb/900g mixed boneless game meat, such as pheasant, pigeon breast, venison, or rabbit
cut into 1/2in/1cm pieces · 2 tbsp brandy · 15oz/450g pork loin, ground
pinch ground cinnamon · pinch ground ginger · 4 tbsp chopped mixed herbs, such as parsley
and thyme · 1/2lb/225g thin strips bacon · salt and ground black pepper

for the jellied stock
2 1/2 cups/600ml jellied stock (see Melton Mowbray Pie, page 117), made using reserved bones
from the game

Heat the butter in a large skillet, add the onion and garlic and cook gently until softened. Remove from the heat and transfer to a large bowl. Stir in the game meat, brandy, pork, cinnamon, ginger, and herbs and season well to taste. Set aside.

Preheat the oven to 400°F. Place a heavy-duty baking sheet in the oven.

Cut off one-third of the pastry and set this aside for the lid. Roll out the larger piece to about 5in/12cm larger than the base of your raised pie mold or pan (you can use an 8in/20cm loose-bottomed cake pan) and use it to line the base and sides, leaving a little excess pastry overhanging the sides. Make sure there are no cracks or holes and that the pastry is evenly distributed around the pan. Roll out the remaining pastry to fit the top of the pie and set aside.

Arrange the strips of bacon in the base of the pastry shell, so that they come up the sides. Pile the game mixture in the center and mound in the middle to support the lid. Brush the overhanging pastry edges with a little beaten egg and then place the pastry lid on top. Pinch and crimp the edges of the shell and lid to seal and trim away any excess pastry. Brush the top with egg to glaze. Use the excess pastry to make leaves to decorate the top. Brush with beaten egg and make a steam hole in the middle of the lid. Place the pie on the hot baking sheet and bake for 30 minutes, then reduce the oven temperature to 325°F and bake for a further 2 hours. Cover the lid with a sheet of aluminum foil if the top starts to brown too quickly.

Warm the jellied stock until melted, then pour in through the steam hole while the pie is still warm. Leave to cool completely before removing the pie from the pan and cutting into slices to serve.

raised fish pie

As fish requires much less cooking than meat, you won't need hot-water crust pastry for this pie. A rich shortcrust pastry, made with a mixture of butter and lard or shortening, makes a great container for the delicate filling. Serve it cold, cut into wedges, with a creamy lemon and herb mayonnaise.

makes a 7in/18cm pie

for the pastry
10oz/300g rich shortcrust pastry (see page 16) · milk, to glaze

for the filling
1lb/450g salmon fillet · 1¹/₄ cups/300ml fish stock · ¹/₂lb/225g smoked salmon · 1 egg, beaten
2 tbsp heavy cream · juice and grated zest of 1 lemon · small bunch flat-leaf parsley, finely
chopped · ground black pepper

Preheat the oven to 400°F. Place a heavy-duty baking sheet in the oven.

Roll out two-thirds of the pastry to make a disk large enough to line the base and sides of a 7in/18cm loose-bottomed cake pan, leaving a ³/₄in/2cm overhang of excess pastry. Roll out the remaining pastry to make a lid. Chill in the refrigerator until needed.

Place the salmon in a deep skillet, pour over the fish stock and bring to a simmer. Poach for 4–5 minutes until the fish flakes easily. Strain well, reserving the stock. Flake the fish into pieces.

Place the smoked salmon in a food processor and whiz with the egg, cream, lemon juice, zest, and parsley. Season with plenty of ground black pepper.

Spread the smoked salmon paste on to the base and sides of your pastry shell and then pile the flaked salmon fillet into the center of the pan.

Brush the edges of the pastry with a little milk and then place the lid on top and pinch and crimp the edges of the shell and lid to seal, trimming away any excess pastry. Brush the top of the pie with the remaining milk and bake for 35 minutes until golden. Pour about 4 tablespoons of the reserved stock into the pie through the steam hole, before allowing the pie to cool.

melton mowbray pork pie

Making a pork pie is not difficult—it just takes time rather than any special skill. It really is worth the effort, as it's immensely satisfying to create something so grand and delicious.

Get your butcher to remove the bones from the pork shoulder so you can keep them for the jellied stock and ask for a pig's foot too, as this really does give the best flavor. You can recognize a true hand-raised Melton Mowbray pie from the way the sides are slightly bowed, where the pie has been baked and then collapsed a little. However, there's a real skill to raising a pie by hand, and to make life easier I use an 8in/20cm loose-bottomed cake pan.

If you're making individual pies, simply shape the pastry for each pie over a jelly jar (as for the Scotch Pies, page 110), wrap it with a strip of baking parchment or waxed paper and tie a piece of string around the middle before removing the shell.

makes 1 x 8in/20cm pie or 6 individual 4in/10cm pies

for the pastry
1lb/500g hot-water crust pastry (see page 21) · beaten egg, to glaze

for the jellied stock
bones from the pork plus 1 pig's foot · 1 large carrot · 1 onion
1 bouquet garni of celery, bay leaf, thyme, and parsley · salt · 12 black peppercorns

for the filling
2lb/900g boned pork shoulder · 1/2lb/250g thick strips bacon · 2 tbsp chopped fresh sage
pinch each ground nutmeg, cinnamon, and allspice · 1 tsp anchovy essence, or to taste

First make the jelly. Put all the ingredients in a large saucepan and cover with 6 cups/1.5 litres of water. Bring to a boil, then put on the lid and cook gently for 2 hours. Strain the stock through a sieve, return to the saucepan and boil rapidly until the liquid has reduced to about 2 1/2 cups/600ml. Season with a little salt and leave to cool. This will keep in the refrigerator for up to 4 days.

For the filling, chop the pork and bacon into 1/2in/1cm pieces. Place half the pork and bacon into a food processor and process, using the pulse button, until coarsely chopped. Transfer to a bowl with the rest of the chopped pork and bacon and mix together with the sage, spices, and anchovy essence.

Cut off one-third of the pastry and set aside for the lid. Roll out the larger piece to a disk about 10¹/₂in/26cm, so that it's large enough to line the base and sides of an 8in/20cm loose-bottomed spring-form cake pan with some pastry overhanging the sides (if you're making individual pies, follow the method for Scotch Pies on page 110). Roll out the remaining pastry to fit the top of the pie.

Preheat the oven to 400°F.

Pack the filling into the pastry shell, mounding it up slightly to support the lid. Moisten the edges of the pastry with beaten egg, lay the lid on top and pinch and crimp the edges of the shell and lid to seal. Trim away any excess pastry, brush with beaten egg and create a hole in the center.

Bake for 30 minutes, then lower the temperature to 325°F and bake for 60 minutes. (If you're making individual pies, bake for 20 minutes at 400°F, then for 50 minutes at 325°F.) Remove the pie from the oven and unclip the outer pan. Brush the pastry with the remaining beaten egg and return to the oven for a further 30 minutes until golden brown.

Allow the pie to cool slightly then heat the jellied stock in a saucepan and slowly pour it into the warm pie, ideally using a funnel. The stock needs to be hot so that it sinks into the filling. Don't hurry this process or you will flood the outer crust of the pie.

Leave the pie to go completely cold overnight before serving it cut into wedges.

veal and ham raised pie

We are probably more familiar with this pie in its mass-produced form. You will know it as the one with the egg that runs through the center. How do they make it so that everyone gets a slice of egg?! That's a mystery we will never know the answer to.

There are many historical recipes for this pie and lots of regional variations. Traditionally it contains veal and cooked ham—a far cry from the manufactured pie, which is made with pork and ham. This version has a wonderful light and flavorsome filling and is certainly worth the time and effort for a special occasion. I love to eat it with pickles, mustard, radish, a tasty, sharp hard cheese, and a glass of strong cider—yum *(illustrated on preceding pages)*.

serves 8

for the pastry
1lb/500g hot-water crust pastry (see page 21) · beaten egg, to glaze

for the filling
1lb/500g stewing veal · 1lb/500g cooked ham · 4 tbsp chopped flat-leaf parsley
grated zest and juice of 1 lemon · 4 hard-cooked eggs, peeled · ground black pepper

for the jellied stock
3/4 cup/200ml jellied stock (see Melton Mowbray Pork Pie, page 117), made in advance

Preheat the oven to 400°F. Place a heavy-duty baking sheet in the oven.

Cut off one-third of the pastry and set this aside for the lid. Roll out the larger piece to an oblong shape large enough to line the base and sides of an approximately 12 x 4 1/2in/30 x 11cm loaf pan, with an overhang of about 3/4in/2cm. Roll out the remaining pastry to fit the top of the pie and set aside.

Chop the veal and ham coarsely into 1/4in/5mm pieces. Place in a bowl and mix with the parsley, lemon zest and juice, and plenty of ground black pepper (the ham will be quite salty, so you won't need to add salt).

Spread a layer of the meat mixture on top of the pastry and arrange the eggs lengthwise, one after the other, down the center of the pan. Cover the eggs with the rest of the meat, pressing down gently.

Brush the edges of the pastry with a little beaten egg. Place the pastry lid on top of the filling and pinch and crimp the edges of the shell and lid to seal, trimming away any excess pastry. Use the pastry trimmings to make decorative leaves. Brush the top of the pie with beaten egg and make a hole in the center. Arrange the pastry leaves on top and brush with egg glaze.

Sit the pie on the baking sheet and bake for 30 minutes, then reduce the oven temperature to 325°F and cook for a further 1 1/2 hours. If the lid starts to brown too quickly, cover the pie with a piece of aluminum foil.

Remove the pie from the oven and leave it to cool for 10 minutes.

Heat the jellied stock and pour it very slowly through a small funnel into the pie. Leave the pie to cool completely before serving it cut into slices.

Mrs King's pork pies

Brothers Paul, Ian, and Neil Harland, who make Mrs King's Pork Pies at Cropwell Bishop in Nottinghamshire, England, really do know and love their product—authentic, hand-raised pork pies made with care. Ever since the first Melton Mowbray pie found popularity as a convenience food for Leicestershire huntsmen to carry in their saddlebags, the pies have been made with fresh rather than cured pork. This is one of the crucial distinctions between Melton Mowbray and other pork pies. Paul, who is a hands-on pie maker *extraordinaire*, insists on

the best locally sourced pork and hand-chops all the fillings. Another distinguishing feature is the pie casing— it must be hot-water crust pastry and baked without any external support such as a pan or hoop. Watching Paul hand-raise the large pork pies, I'm sure that many other manufacturers don't dedicate as much time and effort to their product—most mass-produced pies are now machine-made.

The hand-raised pies are shaped and filled, then baked on sheets until browned and bubbling. A home-made jelly is then poured through the holes and allowed to cool and set. The attention and effort that goes into making

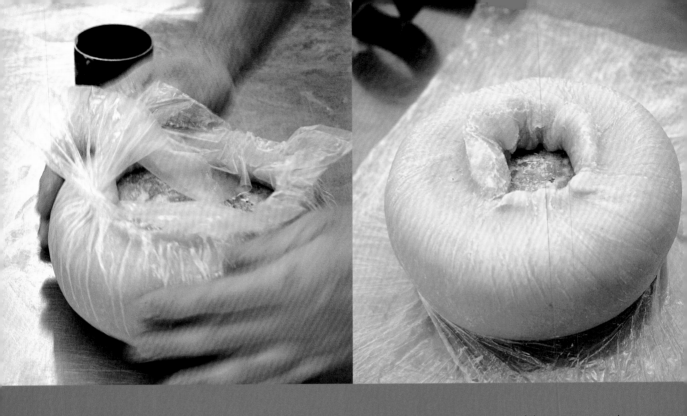

Authentic pork pies, hand-raised with love – you can expect crumbly pastry and firm, fresh-flavoured, succulent filling.

these pies is really shown in the finished result. They are delicious, crisp, and tasty and I can't visit Borough Market in London, where they have a stall, without buying one.

Of the millions of pork pies manufactured in Britain each year only 3 million come from the Melton Mowbray area. Many companies elsewhere in the country add the name Melton Mowbray to their pies because it carries the weight of prestige and quality. Matters, however, are about to change—an application has been made to the European Commission in Brussels for privileged status for authentic Melton Mowbray pies (as already exists for other famous British foods such as Stilton cheese, Newcastle Brown Ale, Whitstable oysters, and Cornish clotted cream). It petitions that only pork pies produced in a clearly defined area in and around the Vale of Belvoir, made with the correct ingredients and by traditional methods, should be allowed to call themselves Melton Mowbray pies. Hopefully this

will end confusion as to the identity of a real Melton Mowbray pie, and when you buy one you can expect crumbly pastry and a firm, fresh-flavored, succulent filling—just as delicious as they claim.

gooseberry raised pie

This is a fantastic old recipe which both tastes amazing and looks rather wonderful. It uses really simple ingredients and is a must when gooseberries are in season. Serve it in wedges with a large dollop of whipped heavy cream, or "clotted cream"—sometimes known as Devonshire or Devon cream.

makes a 6in/15cm pie

for the pastry
1lb/500g hot-water crust pastry (see page 21) · beaten egg, to glaze

for the filling
4 cups trimmed fresh gooseberries · 7oz/200g jar apple jelly
2 tbsp superfine sugar

Preheat the oven to 400°F.

Cut off one-third of the pastry and set this aside for the lid. Roll out the larger piece to create a disk large enough to line the base and sides of a 6in/15cm loose-bottomed cake pan, with an overhang of about 3/4in/2cm. Roll out the remaining pastry to fit the top of the pie.

Fill the pastry shell with the gooseberries, mounding them up in the center to support the lid, and brush the edges of the pastry shell with a little beaten egg. Put on the pastry lid, pinching the edges of the shell and lid to seal and trimming away any excess pastry. Make a small hole in the lid. Brush the top with a little beaten egg and sprinkle with the superfine sugar. Bake the pie for 30 minutes and then reduce the oven temperature to 350°F and cook for a further 30 minutes.

Allow the pie to cool slightly. Place the apple jelly in a small saucepan and heat gently until it is melted and runny, then pour it through the hole in the lid using a small funnel. Allow the pie to cool completely before serving, cut into wedges.

raised venison pie with cranberry glaze

This pie offers a fine combination of flavors—rich port, gamey venison, and sharp cranberry. The glazed cranberry layer makes a great alternative to a pie crust, as well as being the perfect complement to the flavorsome filling.

makes a 7in/18cm square pie

for the pastry
15oz/450g hot-water crust pastry (see page 21)

for the filling
2lb/900g venison neck, breast or shoulder, diced into ³/₄in/2cm cubes · 1¹/₄ cups/300ml red wine or port · ¹/₄ stick/25g butter · 2 shallots, finely chopped · 6 strips bacon, finely chopped 4oz/100g calf's liver, finely chopped · bunch flat-leaf parsley, finely chopped · salt and ground black pepper · 4 tbsp redcurrant jelly · 2 cups/250g fresh or frozen cranberries

for the jellied stock
³/₄ cup/200ml jellied stock (see Melton Mowbray Pork Pie, page 117), made in advance

For the filling, place the venison in a large bowl, pour over the wine and season with a little salt and plenty of ground black pepper. Set aside.

Heat the butter in a large skillet and gently cook the shallots for a few minutes until softened. Add the bacon and liver and cook for a few more minutes until browned all over. Remove from the heat and leave to cool.

Preheat the oven to 400°F. Place a heavy-duty baking sheet in the oven.

Roll out the pastry to a disk large enough to line the base and sides of a 10in/25cm loose-bottomed cake pan with an overhang of about ³/₄in/2cm.

Add the shallot mixture and flat-leaf parsley to the venison, mix together, then spoon into the prepared pie shell. Bake for 2 hours until the meat filling is completely cooked and tender. Allow to cool, then heat the jellied stock in a small saucepan and gently pour in as much stock as the pie will hold, reserving about ¹/₄ cup/50ml for the glaze. Leave to cool and set.

Meanwhile heat the redcurrant jelly in a saucepan, tip in the cranberries and heat through until they begin to soften but still hold their shape. Spoon the cranberries over the top of the pie in a single layer, pour over the remaining jellied stock, and allow to set.

sweetpie

Sweet pies are a truly wonderful thing – the only drawback is that you have to wait for them to cool before eating. The combination of a light, crispy pastry and sweet, juicy, seasonal fruits, creamy chocolate or dried fruits is the pure genius that has kept many of us happy for years.

From the humble apple pie served with a coating of creamy custard to traditional mince pies eaten with a dollop of brandy butter, these are recipes that have really stood the test of time and are still loved today.

The following recipes include a selection of familiar favourites as well as some equally fantastic new ideas. For the ultimate sweet-pie experience – traditional or otherwise – just serve a warm slice of pie on a plate with a liberal helping of custard or cream, or a few scoops of delicious ice cream. Yum!

chocolate-filled pear puddings

Tender pears filled with a chocolate and almond stuffing and wrapped in flaky pastry not only taste amazing but look pretty stunning too. This recipe works equally well with dessert apples.

serves 4

for the pastry
1lb/500g ready-made puff pastry · beaten egg, to glaze

for the filling
2^{1}/$_{2}$oz/70g bittersweet chocolate · 3 tbsp heavy cream · ^{1}/$_{2}$ cup/40g ground almonds
4 tender ripe pears

Preheat the oven to 400°F.

Peel the pears but do not remove the stems. Using a vegetable corer, carefully core each pear from the bottom to within 1in/2.5cm of the top.

Place the chocolate in a small saucepan with the cream and heat very gently until the chocolate has melted. Remove from the heat and stir in the ground almonds. Set aside until cool enough to handle.

Fill the cavity of each pear with the chocolate mixture, pushing it up into the pear using a teaspoon or your thumb.

Roll out the pastry to create a large square sheet, about ^{1}/$_{8}$in/3mm thick and 16in/40cm square. Cut into 4 squares of 8in/20cm. Sit a filled pear in the center of each square and wrap the pastry up and around the pear to cover. You may need to trim away any excess, but you can use this to make pastry leaves for decoration.

Paste any leaves on to the pears using a little water. Place the pears on a parchment-lined baking sheet and chill for about 30 minutes until ready to bake.

Lightly brush each pear with beaten egg to glaze and bake for 20–25 minutes until the pastry is puffed and lightly browned.

pear frangipane croustade

I love frangipane filling—that gooey, chewy texture—and it's especially delicious when combined with the flavor of pears. This recipe is based on the classic almond pie, pithiviers.

serves 8

for the pastry
1lb/500g ready-made puff pastry · beaten egg, to glaze · confectioner's sugar, for dusting

for the filling
8 small ripe pears (tender Comice would be perfect) · grated zest and juice of 1 lemon
1 stick/125g butter, softened · 1 egg · 2 tbsp/30ml dark rum or Cointreau
$^1/_3$ cup/75g superfine sugar · 2 cups/200g ground almonds

Preheat the oven to 400°F.

Peel and core the pears and slice each one into 8 lengthwise. Place the slices in a bowl and toss with the lemon zest and half the lemon juice. Beat the butter in a bowl until softened and then beat in the egg, rum or Cointreau, superfine sugar, ground almonds, and remaining lemon juice.

Cover a large baking sheet with baking parchment paper. Roll out half of the pastry on a lightly floured surface until about $^1/_8$in/3mm thick and cut out a 10$^1/_2$in/27cm disk using a plate as a guide. Lay the pastry on the baking sheet. Spread the almond mixture on the pastry disk up to 1in/2.5cm from the edge. Top with the sliced pears.

Roll out the remaining pastry to an 11in/28cm disk. Brush the edge of the pastry base with beaten egg, then carefully lay the pastry lid over the filling. Press the edges firmly to seal and scallop the edge of the pie decoratively, using a knife to make the indentations.

Brush the top with beaten egg to glaze and use a sharp knife to make faint lines radiating out from the center to the edge in semicircle patterns. Bake for about 30 minutes until well risen and golden. Dust the top generously with confectioner's sugar and serve warm with cream or ice cream.

baby apple calvados pies

These luxurious apple pies are perfect served warm after dinner with a large dollop of sweetened mascarpone. Simply stir confectioner's sugar into some mascarpone and, for extra luxury, add a splash of Calvados.

makes 12 pies

for the pastry
10oz/300g sweet shortcrust pastry (see page 15)

for the filling
2 tbsp/25g butter · 8 sharp apples, such as Granny Smith, peeled, cored, and cut into
1/2in/1cm cubes · 1/3 cup/75g superfine sugar, plus extra for dusting · 1/4 tsp ground cinnamon
grated zest of 1/2 lemon · 3 tbsp Calvados or brandy · 4 tbsp heavy cream

Melt the butter in a saucepan, then add the apples, sugar,
cinnamon, lemon zest, and Calvados. Toss together well in the
pan and cook for 10 minutes until the apples have softened
and you have a coarse purée. Leave to cool, then stir in the
heavy cream.

Preheat the oven to 375°F.

Roll out the pastry on a lightly floured surface to 1/8in/3mm
thick. Using a plain cutter, stamp out 12 disks to line a 12-hole
muffin pan and 12 smaller disks for lids. Line the molds with
the larger disks of pastry and fill with the apple mixture.

Brush the rim of each shell with water and top with the small
disks of pastry. Trim with a knife to make neat edges. Make
3 small neat holes in the top of each pie and dust with sugar.

Bake for 25 minutes until golden at the edges. Allow to cool a little, then remove from the pan,
dust with a little more sugar and serve warm with sweetened mascarpone.

chocolate and pecan pie

This sticky, gooey chocolate pie is perfect served warm with vanilla ice cream. As the filling is quite rich and sweet, a whole pastry lid would be too heavy—the lattice pastry topping is much lighter, as well as looking lovely (*illustrated on preceding pages*).

serves 6

for the pastry
300g/10oz sweet shortcrust pastry (see page 15), with 3¹/₂ tbsp/25g all-purpose flour replaced with unsweetened cocoa powder

for the filling
1 cup/100g light brown sugar · ¹/₂ cup/175g corn syrup · 3 eggs, lightly beaten
2 tsp vanilla extract · 1³/₄ cups/200g roughly chopped pecans · 3oz/75g dark bittersweet chocolate, chopped

Preheat the oven to 350°F.

Grease a 9in/23cm pie dish. Roll out two-thirds of the pastry on a lightly floured surface to about ¹/₈in/3mm thick and 1in/2.5cm bigger than the dish. Place the pastry into the dish and carefully press into the sides. Trim the edges and chill while you make the filling.

Mix together the sugar, syrup, eggs, and vanilla and whisk with a fork. Spread the pecans on the bottom of the pastry shell with the chocolate. Pour the syrup mixture over the nuts and chocolate.

Roll out the remaining pastry and cut into strips to form a lattice topping over the pie. Trim the edges with a knife to neaten.

Bake for 35–40 minutes until the filling is set but gooey and oozing. The filling will be a bit wobbly but will set further on cooling. Cool completely before cutting into wedges to serve.

berry turnovers

These are so simple to make and perfect served warm with extra berry compote and a dollop of cream.

makes 8

for the pastry
10oz/300g rich sweet shortcrust pastry (see page 16)

for the filling
4 cups/500g fresh or frozen mixed berries (defrosted if frozen)
1/4 cup/60g light muscovado sugar · milk for brushing · 1/2 cup/100g superfine sugar
1/2 vanilla pod, split lengthwise, seeds scraped with a knife and reserved

Preheat the oven to 400°F.

Place the berries and sugar in a large saucepan and bring to a simmer. Cook over a gentle heat for 25 minutes until reduced to a thick, pulpy mixture. Remove from the heat and transfer to a bowl and leave to cool.

Divide the pastry into two equal pieces and roll out one at a time to an 8in/20cm square. Cut into four 4in/10cm squares using a fluted pastry wheel.

Spoon a tablespoon of the mixture near the center of each square. Brush the edges with a little milk. Bring the corner of the pastry over the filling to the opposite corner making a little triangle. Seal the edges and repeat with the remaining pastry.

Place the sugar and the vanilla seeds in a small food processor and process until combined. Brush the tops of the turnovers with milk and then sprinkle with the vanilla sugar. Bake for 15 minutes until lightly browned. Transfer to a wire rack to cool. Serve warm with extra berry compote and a dollop of cream.

bakewell pie

This is an old recipe from Derbyshire, England, and I've suggested making it using strawberry or raspberry conserve. You can, however, add fresh fruit to the conserve to transform it into a really superior pie.

serves 6

for the pastry
10oz/300g sweet shortcrust pastry (see page 15)

for the filling
5 tbsp strawberry or raspberry conserve · $^1/_2$ cup/100g raspberries · $^1/_4$ cup/50g butter
$^1/_4$ cup/50g superfine sugar · 1 egg, beaten · $3^1/_2$ tbsp/25g all-purpose flour
$^1/_2$ level tsp baking powder · $^2/_3$ cup/50g ground almonds · 1 tbsp milk

Preheat the oven to 350°F.

Roll out the pastry on a lightly floured surface to a thickness of $^1/8$in/3mm and use it to line an 8in/20cm shallow pie plate, reserving the trimmings. Prick the base and cover it with the conserve and raspberries.

Place the butter and sugar in a large bowl and mix together with an electric mixer or wooden spoon until smooth, light, and fluffy. Add the egg a little at a time, beating thoroughly until incorporated.

Sift together the flour and baking powder, add the ground almonds, and then stir into the egg and sugar mixture, adding the milk to make the mixture soft and creamy. Spread the mixture over the conserve and fruit in the pastry shell and decorate the top with pastry leaves made from the reserved trimmings.

Bake for 30–35 minutes until puffed and golden. Serve warm or at room temperature.

eccles cakes

They're called cakes but technically they're pies—and we love them whatever they are. There are 101 recipes for Eccles cakes, but whether they use lard-based pastry or puff, omit allspice or include nutmeg, they are all sugar-coated, crisp pastries containing dried fruit and a heady old English spice mix. To be really good, they should have a crunchy pastry coating and a moist, dense, highly spiced filling. This version is sure to bring a smile to the lips in the depths of winter.

makes 9

for the pastry
1lb/500g ready-made puff pastry · 1 egg white, lightly whisked, to glaze
1/4 cup/50g demerara sugar

for the filling
1/4 stick + 1 tsp/35g butter
1/4 cup/40g brown sugar
3/4 cup/70g dried currants · 1 tbsp candied peel · 1/2 tsp ground allspice · 1/2 tsp ground nutmeg

Preheat the oven to 50°F.

Roll out the pastry on a lightly floured surface to make a large sheet about 1/8in/3mm thick. Cut out 9 disks about 5in/12cm in diameter. Allow to stand while you make the filling.

Melt the butter and sugar together in a small pan, then stir in the remaining filling ingredients. Place a large tablespoon of filling in the center of each of the pastry disks. Brush the edges of the disk with a little egg white. Working round the disk, take a section of the pastry between your thumb and index finger and fold it into the center. Take the next section and fold it into the center, overlapping the previous fold. Press down to seal it. Continue until you have gathered up all the edges and have formed a package. Flip the package over and, pressing down gently with the palm of your hand, shape it to form a perky-looking, plump oval. Slash the pastry twice on the top, brush with egg white, and sprinkle with demerara sugar.

Place the cakes onto a baking sheet and bake for 15–20 minutes. There is lots of sugar in the filling, so watch out that it doesn't boil out of the pastry.

mrs white's treacle pie

This recipe was given to me by my friend Jenny's mom, who has made this pie forever and was happy to share it. It's a traditional treacle tart and unbelievably simple, but also a delicious classic that we should never forget.

serves 4

for the pastry
7oz/200g sweet shortcrust pastry (see page 15)

for the filling
1 cup/250g English golden syrup or corn syrup · 1 1/2 cups/75g fresh white breadcrumbs
grated zest and juice of 1 lemon

Roll out the pastry on a lightly floured surface to a thickness of 1/8in3/mm and use to line an 8in/20cm pie pan. Trim off any overhanging pastry and chill the pastry shell for 20 minutes. Reserve the pastry trimmings for the top.

Preheat the oven to 400°F. Place a baking sheet in the oven to heat.

Place the golden syrup in a saucepan and heat through. Remove from the heat and stir in the breadcrumbs, lemon zest, and lemon juice. Spread the mixture evenly into the pastry shell.

Roll out the reserved trimmings and cut into 10–12 strips. Twist the strips into spirals and then lay half of them over the pie filling. Arrange the remaining strips at right angles to the first strips to form a lattice. Press the ends of the strips on to the rim of the pastry shell.

Place the pie on the hot baking sheet and bake for 10 minutes. Lower the temperature of the oven to 375°F and bake for a further 15 minutes. Serve warm with stirring custard or cream.

apple and blackberry pie

Deep fruit pies made in earthenware dishes with a single crust are great for using up seasonal fruit when it is plentiful. Pack the fruit well into the dish, piling it high with only a little liquid or it will sink and the crust will fall (a pie funnel will also help to prevent this). Apple and blackberry has got to be the best fruit pie combination ever, but feel free to use whatever is in season and plentiful (*illustrated on preceding pages*).

serves 6

for the pastry
10oz/300g sweet shortcrust pastry (see page 15) · 2 tbsp milk, to glaze

for the filling
$^1/_4$ stick/25g butter · $^1/_2$ tsp ground cinnamon · 1$^1/_2$ cups/325g superfine sugar
1$^1/_2$lb/700g fresh blackberries · 1$^1/_2$lb/700g dessert apples, peeled, cored and sliced

Preheat the oven to 400°F.

Heat the butter in a large saucepan, add the cinnamon, 1$^1/_3$ cups/300g of the sugar, reserving the remainder, and half the blackberries and simmer for about 10 minutes until the fruit is soft. Mash with a potato masher to make a thickish sauce.

Mix the apples and remaining blackberries together and place them in 6 cup/1.5 litre deep pie dish and pour over the blackberry sauce. Place a pie funnel in the center of the filling.

Roll out the pastry on a lightly floured surface to about $^1/_8$in/3mm and 1in/3cm larger than the pie dish. Cut off a strip and press this on to the edge of the dish. Place the pastry lid on top and press down to seal. Trim away any excess pastry, brush the top with milk to glaze and sprinkle with the remaining superfine sugar.

Bake for 30 minutes until the crust is golden and the filling bubbling. Leave to stand for 10–15 minutes before serving with cream.

apple pie with cheese pastry

Apple pie without the cheese is like a kiss without a squeeze.

This is an old Saxon proverb and they certainly knew what they were talking about. This pure apple pie is complemented by the best ever pastry. The old combination of cheese and apple makes absolute sense and, believe me, is wonderful. Use Cox's or Braeburn apples for flavor and because they hold their shape and a good cooking apple to make the delicious sauce.

serves 6

for the pastry
23/4 cups/350g all-purpose flour · 2/3 cup/150g superfine sugar · 11/4 sticks/150g butter, cubed
2 egg yolks · 1/2 cup/50g finely grated mature Cheddar cheese

for the filling
4 large cooking apples, peeled, cored, and chopped (about 2lb/900g) · 1/2lb/250g Cox's or Braeburn apples, peeled, cored, and chopped · 2/3 cup/150g superfine sugar, plus extra for dusting
juice of 1/2 lemon

Place the flour in a large mixing bowl, make a well in the center and tip in the sugar. Add the butter and use your fingertips to rub it into the flour and sugar until the mixture resembles fine breadcrumbs. Stir in the egg yolks and cheese, adding a little water if the mixture seems too dry. Use your hands to form the mixture into a smooth dough. Wrap the dough in plastic wrap and chill for 20 minutes.

Place the apples in a saucepan with the sugar, lemon juice, and 2 tbsp water and cook for about 15 minutes until softened. Leave to cool.

Preheat the oven to 375°F. Place a sturdy baking sheet in the oven to heat.

Roll out two-thirds of the pastry to 1/4in/5mm thick to fit a 9in/23cm pie pan or plate. Fill with the cooled apple mixture. Roll out the remaining pastry to make the lid. Brush the edges of the pastry shell with water and top with the lid, pressing down to seal. Trim with a knife to make a neat edge and crimp the edges with your fingertips, if you like. Make a hole in the top of the pastry and dust with superfine sugar. Place on the baking sheet and bake for 25–30 minutes until golden. Leave to stand for about 15 minutes before cutting into wedges and serving with cream.

spiced summer berry free-form pie with lemon pastry

This is a pie to make when summer berries are at their plumpest and most flavorsome and it can be adapted to whatever berries you have at hand. The pie takes no time at all—great for hot days, when you don't want to overheat the kitchen or yourself. Serve it with vanilla ice cream for an exquisite taste of summer. The fruit liqueur adds a richness and depth to the sauce created by the berries but it is completely optional. A good squeeze of fresh orange over the berries works well as an alternative.

serves 4

for the pastry
10oz/300g sweet rich shortcrust pastry (see page 16), adding grated zest of 1 lemon to the mixture

for the filling
1/4 stick/25g butter, melted · 1/2 cup/50g light brown sugar, plus extra for sprinkling
1 1/4lb/625g mixed summer berries, such as raspberries, blueberries, strawberries
1 tbsp cornstarch · pinch ground cinnamon · 3 tbsp crème de cassis or any fruit liqueur

Preheat the oven to 400°F.

Place the melted butter in a large bowl and toss with the brown sugar, mixed berries, cornstarch, cinnamon, and crème de cassis.

On a lightly floured surface, roll out the pastry to fit a 10in/25cm ceramic dish, allowing about 1 1/2in/4cm excess pastry to hang over the edges.

Spoon the berry mixture into the pastry shell and fold the excess pastry up over the fruit, overlapping as needed and leaving the center open. Brush with milk and sprinkle with sugar.

Bake for 30 minutes until the crust is golden brown and the juices are bubbling. Serve warm with vanilla ice cream.

strawberry and rhubarb cobbler

A cobbler is a kind of pie in an unofficial kind of way and it's such a great dessert that I felt it would be a shame not to include at least one.

The biscuit-like topping is spooned over the filling rather than rolled out, which makes it easy to make. It's perfect for soaking up all the juices from the filling. Tart, crisp, tasty rhubarb and smooth, sweet strawberries are naturally complementary.

serves 6

for the cobbler topping
2 cups/225g all-purpose flour · pinch salt · 3 tsp baking powder · 1 tsp ground cinnamon
1 stick/100g chilled butter, cut into pieces · 3/4 cup/175ml buttermilk · 3 tbsp milk

for the filling
1 3/4lb/900g fresh rhubarb stalks, trimmed of any leaves and cut into 3/4in/2cm lengths
1lb/500g fresh strawberries, hulled and sliced · 2/3 cup/150g superfine sugar · 1 tbsp cornstarch
grated zest and juice of 1 orange · 1/2 tsp ground ginger

Preheat the oven to 400°F.

Place the rhubarb and strawberries, sugar, cornstarch, orange zest, juice, and ginger in the base of an 8 cup/2 litre deep pie dish and toss well to combine.

To make the topping, place the flour in a large bowl and mix with the salt, baking powder, and cinnamon. Add the butter and rub into the flour mixture with your fingertips until the mixture resembles fine breadcrumbs. Stir in the buttermilk and milk to make a thick batter mixture.

Drop tablespoons of the batter mixture on top of the fruit to cover the entire surface, creating a "cobbled" effect, and bake for 35–40 minutes until the topping is golden and the filling bubbling.

chocolate and pistachio cream pie

This pie has a deliciously creamy chocolate custard filling which is so simple to make, and it's perfect served warm with scoops of vanilla ice cream. Bake it in a rectangular baking pan so that it's really easy to slice into bars *(illustrated on preceding pages)*.

serves 6

for the pastry
10oz/300g sweet shortcrust pastry (see page 15), adding grated zest of 1 orange to the mixture
2 tbsp milk, to glaze

for the filling
2 eggs · 2/3 cup/150g superfine sugar, plus extra for sprinkling · 2/3 cup/150ml heavy cream
5oz/150g bittersweet dark chocolate, finely chopped · 2 tbsp pistachio nuts, toasted and
roughly chopped

Preheat the oven to 350°F.

Lightly grease a fluted 14 x 4 1/2in/36 x 11cm baking pan. Divide the dough into 2 portions, one slightly larger than the other. Roll the larger portion out to a rectangle big enough to line the base and sides of the pan. Cover with plastic wrap and chill in the refrigerator while you make the filling. Roll out the remaining pastry to a size large enough to cover the top of the pan. Place on a baking sheet, cover with plastic wrap, and also chill while you prepare the filling.

Place the eggs and sugar in a bowl and beat together. Stir in the cream, chocolate, and pistachio nuts, then pour into the pastry shell. Brush the rim of the pastry with milk and position the lid in place, pressing the edges to seal. Trim the edges and make a steam hole in the middle of the lid. Brush with milk to glaze and sprinkle with superfine sugar.

Bake for 30–35 minutes, then leave to cool for at least 15 minutes before removing from the pan. Place on a cooling rack and leave to cool for a further 10 minutes before cutting into slices. Letting the pie stand for a few minutes allows it to set, making it easier to slice. Don't worry—it will still be warm and gooey!

custard cream pie

A far cry from the slapstick custard pies! This is a rich and luscious filling which sets perfectly to be able to slice into perfect wedges.

serves 6

for the pastry
10oz/300g rich sweet shortcrust (pastry see page 16)

for the filling
3 large eggs · ²/₃ cup/125g superfine sugar · 300ml/¹/₂ pint full-fat milk · 1¹/₄ cups/300ml heavy cream   1 vanilla pod split lengthwise, seeds scraped with a knife and reserved ·
1 tbsp granulated sugar

Preheat the oven to 400°F.

Roll out the pastry to fit an 8in/20cm pie pan or dish. Press the pastry into the pan, trimming away the excess and place in the refrigerator to chill for 15 minutes.

Line the pastry shell with parchment paper and fill with pie weights or dried beans. Bake for 10 minutes, then remove the weights and paper and bake for another 10 minutes until golden.

Reduce the oven temperature to 300°F. Whisk the eggs and sugar in a large bowl. Pour the milk, cream and vanilla pod and seeds into a saucepan and bring to a boil. Pour onto the eggs (removing the vanilla pod), whisking as you go.

Pour the custard mixture into the baked pie shell right to the top and sprinkle with the granulated sugar. Place carefully in the oven and bake for 50 minutes. When it is ready, the filling should be set and golden on top and have the slightest tremor in the center when you jiggle the pan. Cool completely, then serve in slices.

raspberry cream pies

These coconut-custard-and-fresh-raspberry-filled pies are a far cry from any slapstick custard version. They're far too good for throwing—serve them warm or cold alongside some extra berries on a plate.

makes 6 pies

for the pastry
10oz/300g sweet shortcrust pastry (see page 15)

for the filling
$^2/_3$ cup/150ml heavy cream · 1 cup/250ml coconut milk · $^2/_3$ cup/150g superfine sugar
1 egg · grated zest of 1 lime · generous cup/200g fresh raspberries

Roll out the pastry on a lightly floured surface to about $^1/_8$in/3mm thick. Cut out 4 disks large enough to line 4 individual pie pans, 4in/10cm in diameter. From the remaining pastry, cut out wide strips to make covers for the tops.

Press the pastry into the base and sides of each pan and prick the base with a fork. Fill with a ball of scrunched-up aluminum foil (to weigh down the pastry during cooking). Chill for at least 20 minutes before baking to stop the pastry shrinking.

Preheat the oven to 325°F. Place a baking sheet in the oven to heat.

Place the pies on the hot baking sheet and bake for 7 minutes. Meanwhile mix together the cream, coconut milk, sugar, egg, and lime zest in a large bowl.

Remove the foil from the pastry shells and divide the raspberries between the pies. Pour over the cream mixture and cover with the strips of pastry—you can be as creative as you like, either making a lattice topping or arranging the strips decoratively in a random pattern. Press the strips onto the edges to seal and trim away any excess pastry.

Bake the pies for 20–25 minutes until the crust is golden and the filling is nearly set but still creamy and wobbly. Leave to cool in the pans for about 15 minutes before removing and serve warm or cold with extra berries.

peach and apricot amaretti pie

This is a pie to make at the peak of the peach season. Amaretto flavoring has a great affinity with peaches and apricots and I have used crushed Amaretti cookies in the filling for added texture and sprinkled finely crushed biscuits on top to provide a crunchy finish.

serves 6

for the pastry
10oz/300g sweet shortcrust pastry (see page 15) · 2 tbsp milk, to glaze

for the filling
14oz/400g fresh apricots, halved, pitted and cut into wedges · 1lb/500g fresh peaches, halved, pitted and cut into wedges · 2/3 cup/150g superfine sugar, plus extra for dusting
3 tbsp Amaretto liqueur · 3 tbsp cornstarch · 2 tsp lemon juice · 4 Amaretti cookies, finely crushed · 1 tbsp butter, cut into pieces

Preheat the oven to 400°F.

Place the apricots and peaches in a bowl with the sugar, Amaretto liqueur, cornstarch, lemon juice, and half the Amaretti cookies. Mix together well and set aside while you prepare the pastry.

When your dough is ready, spoon the filling into the base of a 6 cup/1.5 litre pie dish or pan and dot pieces of butter on the top.

On a lightly floured surface, roll out the pastry to just larger than the pie dish, then cut off a strip to sit on the edge of the dish. Place the pastry on top and press down to seal. Trim off any excess pastry and glaze the top with a little milk. Bake for 30 minutes until the crust is golden and the filling bubbling. While the pie is still hot, sprinkle on the remaining crushed Amaretti cookies and superfine sugar. Leave to stand for about 10–15 minutes before serving with fresh pouring (light) cream.

lemon curd and jam pies

We all remember these pies from childhood—simple pastry shells filled with your favorite jam, preserve, or creamy lemon curd *(illustrated on preceding pages)*.

makes 12

for the pastry
10oz/300g sweet shortcrust pastry (see page 15)

for the filling
2 eggs, beaten · 1 cup/200g superfine sugar · 1¼ sticks/150g unsalted butter · grated zest and juice of 2 lemons · red jam or preserve

To make the lemon curd filling, place the beaten eggs in a saucepan, add the sugar, butter, lemon zest, and juice and stir over a gentle heat until the butter and sugar have melted. Continue to cook, stirring all the time, until the mixture thickens—this will take about 20 minutes. Make sure that the mixture doesn't boil during this time as the eggs will curdle. Set aside to cool.

Pour the cooled lemon curd into clean, sterilized jelly jars and store in the refrigerator until required. It will keep for up to 3 weeks

Preheat the oven to 400°F.

To make the pies, roll out the pastry on a lightly floured surface until it is about ⅛in/3mm thick. Cut out 12 disks of 3in/8cm diameter and place them on a baking sheet. Cut out a further 12 disks of the same size (you may have to reroll the pastry for this) and then use a heart- or star-shaped cutter (or whatever takes your fancy) to cut out a shape from the center of these disks. Place these on another baking sheet.

Place both sheets in the oven and bake for 8–12 minutes until the pastry is pale golden. Leave to cool on the sheet for a few minutes, then remove using a spatula and place on a rack to cool completely.

Spread half the disks with lemon curd and top with, for example, the star-shaped lids. Spread the other half with your favorite red jam and top with the remaining lids. Serve dusted with confectioner's sugar.

Yorkshire curd pies

These small pies are like yummy little cheesecakes. Their distinguishing characteristic is the addition of allspice which gives them a superb flavor without being too sweet.

makes 24

for the pastry
10oz/300g sweet shortcrust pastry (see page 15)

for the filling
1 cup/200g cottage cheese · 2 eggs, separated · $1/3$ cup/75g superfine sugar · 2 tbsp heavy cream grated zest and juice of 1 lemon · large pinch ground allspice · $1/2$ cup/50g raisins

Preheat the oven to 350°F.

Roll out the pastry on a lightly floured surface to a thickness of about $1/8$in/3mm. Cut out 24 disks using a $3^1/2$in/7.5cm cookie cutter and use to line shallow muffin pans. Chill the pastry while you prepare the filling.

Place the cottage cheese in a bowl and mix in the egg yolks, sugar, cream, lemon zest, juice, and allspice, then stir in the raisins.

Beat the egg whites until stiff and fold into the cheese mixture. Spoon the filling into the pastry shells and bake for 30–35 minutes until just turning golden.

Serve warm or cold.

apple baklava pie

This is based on the classic recipe for Baklava, but it has apple grated into the mixture. It is delicious served with extra honey drizzled over the top.

serves 9

for the filling
1 stick/125g butter, melted · 1 1/2 cups/200g pistachio nuts · generous 1 cup/170g dried cranberries · 1/2 tsp cinnamon · 1/2 tsp ground ginger · 3 dessert apples, peeled, cored, and grated · 1/2 cup/45g light muscovado sugar · 8 large sheets phyllo pastry

to serve
fresh figs · Greek yogurt · honey

Preheat the oven to 350°F.

Brush a 10in/25cm square cake pan with a little of the butter. Place the pistachios, cranberries, cinnamon, and ginger in a food processor and process until finely chopped. Transfer to a bowl and stir in the grated apple and muscovado sugar.

Place the phyllo pastry on a clean work surface. Cover with a damp dish towel (this prevents it from drying out). Take 1 sheet, brush it with melted butter, and fold to fit into the base of the pan—repeat with 3 more sheets of the phyllo, brushing each one with butter before layering.

Sprinkle the fruit mixture over the pastry and then cover with the remaining buttered phyllo sheets. Tuck the pastry into the sides of the pan. Score the pastry into 9 squares. Bake for 55 minutes until crisp. Serve with fresh figs, a dollop of Greek yogurt and a drizzle of honey.

pumpkin pie

A pie book just wouldn't be complete without a recipe for pumpkin pie. Again, there are many variations on the ultimate recipe but the theme is always the same. Sweet firm pumpkin combined with eggs and cream for a creamy texture, and sugar and spices for comforting flavor.

serves 6

for the pastry
10oz/300g sweet shortcrust pastry (see page 15)

for the filling
1³/₄lb/800g pumpkin, peeled and cubed weight · 2 eggs, lightly beaten
¹/₄ cup/185g light muscovado sugar · ¹/₂ cup/100ml heavy cream · 1 tbsp brandy
¹/₂ tsp ground ginger · ¹/₂ tsp ground nutmeg · 1 tsp ground cinnamon

Preheat the oven to 350°F. Place a heavy baking sheet in the oven.

Place the pumpkin in a large saucepan and cover with water. Bring to a boil and simmer for 15–20 minutes until very tender.

Drain and return to the pan. Mash with a potato masher until you have a smooth purée or push through a large strainer into a bowl for a very smooth mixture. Allow to cool.

On a lightly floured surface, roll out the pastry to about ¹/₈in/3mm thick, then use it to line a 9in/23cm pie dish or pan. Trim off any excess and prick the base with a fork. Crumple a sheet of aluminum foil and place it in the pastry shell to weigh it down then place the dish on the hot baking sheet. Bake for just 10 minutes to set the pastry.

Whisk the eggs and sugar together in a large bowl. Add the cooled pumpkin, cream, brandy, and the spices and stir thoroughly. Pour the mixture into the pastry shell and bake for 40 minutes. Cover randomly with pastry leaves or strips and bake for a further 20 minutes or until set.

As their name suggests, these pies were originally made with minced (ground) or shredded meat. It wasn't until the 18th century that they began to be made with a mix of candied fruits and suet—what we know as mincemeat today.

makes 18 small pies

for the pastry
1³/4 cups/200g all-purpose flour · 1 tsp ground cinnamon · ¹/2 cup/100g superfine sugar
²/3 cup/50g ground almonds · 1 stick/125g butter · 1 egg yolk, beaten plus beaten egg, to glaze

for the mincemeat (makes about 1¹/2 cups/450g)
1 cup/100g raisins · 1 cup/100g golden raisins · ¹/4 cup/50g chopped mixed candied peel
¹/3 cup/90ml whiskey · ¹/2 cup/50g chopped walnuts · 1 tsp cinnamon · 1 tsp nutmeg
1 cup/200g demerara sugar · 2 dessert apples, such as Braeburn or Granny Smith's, peeled, cored, and grated · ¹/2 cup/100g shredded vegetable suet or shortening

To make the mincemeat, roughly chop the raisins and golden raisins and mix with the peel, whiskey, walnuts, cinnamon, nutmeg, sugar, and apples. Leave to stand in a cool place for 48 hours in a bowl covered with plastic wrap. Stir in the suet and spoon the mixture into sterilized jars. Store until required.

Put the flour, cinnamon, sugar, and ground almonds in a bowl. Add the butter and, using your fingertips, gently rub it into the mixture until it resembles breadcrumbs. Make a well in the center and add the egg yolk and about 4 tbsp of cold water. Mix with your fingertips or a knife to form a dough. Knead gently and shape into a ball. Wrap in plastic wrap and chill for 1 hour in the refrigerator before using.

Preheat the oven to 400°F.

For the pies, roll out the pastry on a lightly floured surface to a thickness of about ¹/8in3/mm (if it starts to stick, roll it out between 2 sheets of baking parchment). Cut out 18 disks measuring 3¹/2in/8cm wide and 18 measuring 3in/7cm (for lids). Use the larger disks to line the holes of an 18-hole muffin pan. Put a spoonful of mincemeat in each shell. Add a little extra whiskey if you like. Don't use too much filling or it will boil over and burn the pies. Dampen the edges of the pastry with a little water and top with a lid. Seal the edges, brush the tops with beaten egg, and cut one or two slits in the top of each pie. Bake in the center of the oven for 15–20 minutes until golden. Leave to cool for 10 minutes in the pan before transferring to a rack to cool. Dust the tops with confectioner's sugar before serving.

whisky-laced mince pies

banana, chocolate, and salted caramel pie

This is my updated version of the wonderful Banana Caramel Pie. Just when you thought it couldn't be topped—try it! The banana and caramel make it rich, and it has chocolate, too!

serves 8–12

for the pastry
10oz/300g sweet shortcrust pastry (see page 15), replacing 3¹/₂ tbsp/25 g of the flour with unsweetened cocoa powder and adding ¹/₃ cup/50g of confectioner's sugar

for the filling
1 cup plus 2 tbsp/225g granulated sugar · 1¹/₄ sticks/150g salted butter, cubed · pinch sea salt
7 tbsp crème fraiche · 7oz/200g semisweet chocolate · 2 large or 2 medium ripe bananas, sliced ·
1¹/₄ cups heavy cream · 3 tbsp/25g finely chopped salted pistachios

Preheat the oven to 400°F. Place a baking sheet in the oven to preheat. To make the filling, dissolve the sugar in ¹/₄ cup/60ml of water in a heavy saucepan or skillet over a low heat. Increase the heat until the syrup turns a deep amber color. Swirl the pan occasionally to cook the caramel evenly but don't stir or the sugar will crystallize. Remove from the heat, leave to cool for 1–2 minutes, then stir in 1 stick/120g of the butter with a pinch of sea salt. Whisk in 4 tablespoons of crème fraiche beating until smooth and glossy. Transfer to a bowl and leave to cool for 15 minutes until thickened.

Heat the chocolate, the remaining crème fraiche, and the remaining butter in a heatproof bowl over a saucepan of gently simmering water until melted and smooth. Set aside to cool.

Roll out the pastry on a lightly floured surface to ¹/₄in/5mm thick and 12¹/₂in/32cm diameter. Use to line a 9in/23cm fluted tart pan leaving the excess pastry to overhang the sides. Prick the base with a fork and line with parchment paper and pie weights or dried beans. Chill in the refrigerator for at least 15 minutes. Once chilled, place the pastry shell on the preheated baking sheet and bake for 10 minutes. Remove the paper and weights and bake for another 10–15 minutes until cooked through. Trim off the excess pastry and leave to cool. Remove from the tart shell and cool completely on a wire rack.

Once cooled, arrange the bananas on the pastry base. Loosely swirl the caramel with the chocolate and spoon on top of the bananas. Whip the cream until soft peaks form. Spoon into a pastry bag with a large star-shaped tip. Pipe swirls around the pie edge and sprinkle pistachios on the cream.

cherry custard jalousie pie

A jalousie is a puff pastry pie with slits cut in the pastry top to allow for the fruit to bubble through. This recipe uses a sublime combination of cherries and a custard filling, but you could try any seasonal fruit.

serves 6–8

for the pastry
1lb/500g ready-made puff pastry (or see page 20 for homemade rough puff pastry)

for the filling
scant 1 cup/200ml heavy cream · 1¼ cups/300ml whole milk · 4 egg yolks · ⅔ cup/125g superfine sugar · ½ tsp vanilla extract · 2 tbsp instant custard powder · all-purpose flour for dusting · 2½ cups/400g/13oz pitted fresh or 1½ cups/400g frozen pitted cherries, defrosted milk for glazing · 1 tbsp granulated sugar

For the custard filling, place the cream and milk in a saucepan over a medium heat and bring to a simmer. Place the egg yolks, superfine sugar, vanilla extract, and custard powder in a large bowl and whisk together until smooth. Pour the hot milk and cream over the egg mixture, whisking continuously. Leave to cool.

Preheat the oven to 400°F. Place a baking sheet in the oven to preheat. Cut the puff pastry in half and roll one piece out to about 13 x 7in/33 x 18cm on a lightly floured surface. Carefully place into a rectangular pan measuring 12 x 6in/30 x 15cm and about 1¼in/3cm deep. Prick the base all over with a fork. Spread the cooled custard into the pan and arrange the cherries on top.

Roll out the remaining piece of pastry to a 12 x 6in/30 x 15cm rectangle. Brush the edges with a little milk and lay the other sheet of pastry over the top of the filling and press down gently to seal.

Brush the top with more milk and sprinkle with the granulated sugar. Place the pan in the refrigerator to chill for 15 minutes.

Before placing in the oven make incisions in the pastry with a sharp knife to reveal the filling. Place the baking pan on the preheated baking sheet and bake for 10 minutes, then reduce the temperature to 325°F and continue to bake for another 45 minutes until the pastry is golden and cooked through.

Leave to cool for 10 minutes before removing from the pan. Serve warm or cold cut into squares.

candied ricotta pie

The filling in this pie is based around the wonderful Sicilian cannoli pastry desserts. You can buy candied fruits from speciality food stores and delis—they're definitely worth searching for.

serves 8–12

for the pastry
13oz/400g sweet shortcrust pastry (see page 15) · all-purpose flour for dusting

for the filling
1lb/500g fresh ricotta · $^1/_3$ cup/80g superfine sugar · 1 tsp vanilla extract · 3 extra-large eggs
$^1/_2$ cup/100g candied fruits · $^1/_4$ cup/50g semisweet chocolate chips · $^1/_3$ cup/50g raisins
grated zest 1 lemon · 1 tbsp confectioner's sugar for dusting

Preheat the oven to 350°F. Place a baking pan in the oven to preheat.

Roll out two-thirds of the pastry on a lightly floured surface to make a $^1/_4$in/5mm thick disk. Use to line a 1$^3/_4$in/3.5cm deep, 9in/23cm fluted tart pan, leaving any excess to overhang the pan.

Roll out the remaining pastry on a lightly floured surface to $^1/_4$in/5mm thick. Using a fluted ravioli wheel, cut the dough into $^3/_4$in/2cm strips.

Place the ricotta in a food processor and process until smooth. Transfer to a large bowl and, using a wooden spoon, beat in the sugar, vanilla extract, and eggs, one at a time, until combined.

Stir in the candied fruits, chocolate chips, raisins, and lemon zest. Pour into the pastry shell and arrange half the strips at 1$^1/_2$in/4cm intervals across the top of the pie. Repeat crosswise with the remaining strips to make a lattice topping. Press the edges to seal and trim any excess.

Place on the preheated baking sheet on the lowest oven shelf and bake for 55 minutes until golden. Set aside for 15 minutes to cool in the pan before transferring to a wire rack to cool completely. Dust with confectioner's sugar and serve cut into wedges.

key lime meringue-topped pie

A classic recipe from the Florida Keys. There are many variations on this recipe but the essential ingredients are always condensed milk and lots of fresh lime zest and juice. A really great alternative to the famous lemon meringue pie. However, if lemon really is your favorite then simply replace the lime with equal quantities of lemon juice and zest.

serves 6

for the pastry
10oz/300g sweet shortcrust pastry (see page 15)

for the filling
1¹/₃ cups/400g canned condensed milk · 4 extra-large eggs, separated · zest and juice 4 limes
¹/₂ cup/100g superfine sugar · ¹/₂ tsp cream of tartare

Preheat the oven to 350°F 4. Place a baking sheet in the oven to preheat.

Line a 9in/23cm pie pan or pie plate with the pastry and place in the refrigerator to chill for about 15 minutes. Line with a sheet of parchment paper, add pie weights or dried beans, and bake for 10 minutes. Remove the paper and weights and bake for another 5 minutes.

Meanwhile, whisk the condensed milk and egg yolks together in a bowl, then gradually whisk in the lime juice. Pour the mixture into the pastry shell and bake for 15–20 minutes until the filling is set. Using an electric mixer, beat the egg whites until they form firm peaks, then gradually add the sugar, a tablespoon at a time, constantly whisking. Finally, add the cream of tartare and whisk until you have a stiff, glossy meringue mixture.

Spoon the meringue over the filling, forming peaks with the mixture using the back of a metal spoon. Bake for 7–10 minutes until lightly golden and the meringue is set. Leave to cool slightly before slicing into wedges.

individual blueberry pies with streusel topping

Streusel is the German term meaning 'something scattered or sprinkled'. Rather like a crumble mixture. It gives a great topping to these pies especially with the addition of crumbled Amaretti cookies for extra crunch and flavor.

makes 4 pies

for the pastry
10oz/300g sweet shortcrust pastry (see page 15)

for the filling
¹/₄ cup/50g light muscovado sugar · 2³/₄ cups/400g fresh blueberries
grated zest and juice ½ orange

for the streusel topping
1 cup/125g all-purpose flour · ¹/₄ cup/50g superfine sugar · 6 tbsp/75g unsalted butter, cubed
2 amaretti cookies, crushed

Preheat the oven to 350°F.

Roll out the pastry to ¹/₄in/5mm thick and use to line 4 individual 5¹/₂in/14cm diameter pie pans or deep tart pans.

In a bowl, combine the sugar with the blueberries, orange zest, and 1 tablespoon of orange juice. Spoon the blueberries into the individual pastry shells, filling to the top.

For the topping, place the flour in a bowl and add the sugar. Add the butter and roughly mix into the flour mixture until you have large crumbs. Mix in the crushed amaretti. Sprinkle this over the blueberry filling, covering completely, piling the mixture high.

Place on the preheated baking sheet and bake for 20 minutes until the tops begin to brown. Reduce the oven temperature to 325°F and bake for another 35 minutes until the topping is golden and the filling is bubbling. Perfect served with cream, ice cream or custard.

extrapie

Simple accompaniments are all you need to go with your lovingly prepared pies. Creamy mash, traditional gravy, and mushy peas are the perfect complement to a rich savory pie, while an apple pie is nothing without a generous coating of hot stirring custard. If you've gone to great lengths to make the perfect pie, you'll want to give it that little extra something to complete the finished result.

mushy peas

Traditionally served with fish and chips, mushy peas are a great favorite of mine and lots of others in northern England. During my pie investigations it became apparent that this humble side dish is also a favorite accompaniment to savory pies. From soccer pies to gourmet pies, a spoonful of mushy peas on the side seems to be essential.

serves 4

1 1/3 cups/225g dried marrowfat peas · 1/2 tsp baking of soda
1/4 stick/25g unsalted butter · salt and freshly ground black pepper

Place the peas in a large bowl with the bicarbonate of soda, cover with water, and soak overnight or for at least 4 hours.

Drain the peas and rinse them well in a strainer under cold running water. Place in a saucepan and cover with cold water. Bring to a boil and then reduce the heat to a simmer f or 1–1 1/2 hours, stirring from time to time, until the peas are cooked and have collapsed to a softened mush.

If the peas appear too wet, continue to cook them over a low heat to dry off the excess moisture, but make sure you keep stirring to prevent them burning on the base of the pan.

Beat in the butter, salt, and ground black pepper.

mashed potato

It is essential to ser ve mashed potatoes with meat pies that ha ve a rich gravy, as the potato helps to soak up all the delicious liquid. Simple mash is all you need, using a good mealy potato to give a soft creamy texture.

serves 4

2lb/1kg potatoes, peeled and quartered · good pinch salt and ground black pepper
1/2 stick/50g butter · 2/3 cup/150ml pint hot milk

Place the potatoes in a colander and r inse them under cold running water.

Transfer them to a large saucepan, add a good pinch of salt and co ver with water. Bring to a boil and cook for 15 minutes until tender. Try not to overcook them as they will become water logged and lose their flavor and texture.

Drain well and return to the pan over a low heat for a minute or two to dry out. Mash well, either by hand with a potato masher or with a potato r icer. Add the butter to the mashed potatoes, then the hot milk and mash well together until smooth and creamy. Check the seasoning and add a good grinding of black pepper.

gravy

A jug of rich brown gravy is perfect for serving with meat pies such as the family Meat and Potato Pie (page 40) and the individual Scotch Pies (page 112). It is, of course, easy to use an instant gravy mix but this really won't do justice to your wonderful pie with its home-made pastry and top-quality filling. This gravy is something a little special and not difficult to make at all.

makes about 2 cups/450ml

2 tbsp vegetable oil · 4 cups/500g mixture of diced onion, celery, carrot, and leek 2 garlic cloves, peeled and finely chopped · 2 tsp all-purpose flour · 2/3 cup/150ml red wine 1 3/4 cups/400ml chicken, beef, or lamb stock · salt and freshly ground black pepper

Heat the oil in a large saucepan over a medium heat, add the vegetables and fry for about 30 minutes, stirring occasionally, until they are very dark brown in color (this is your gravy browning). Add the garlic and cook for a further 5 minutes. Sprinkle over the flour and stir it in, then gradually stir in the red wine and cook for a couple of minutes until the gravy starts to thicken. Stir in the stock in two or three batches, add some seasoning and simmer for about 5 minutes.

Pass the gravy through a sieve, pressing out as much liquid as possible from the vegetables as this is where all the flavor is.

Return the gravy to the pan and simmer gently for 10 minutes to reduce the liquid further and to create a smooth glossy gravy. Taste and adjust the seasoning if necessary.

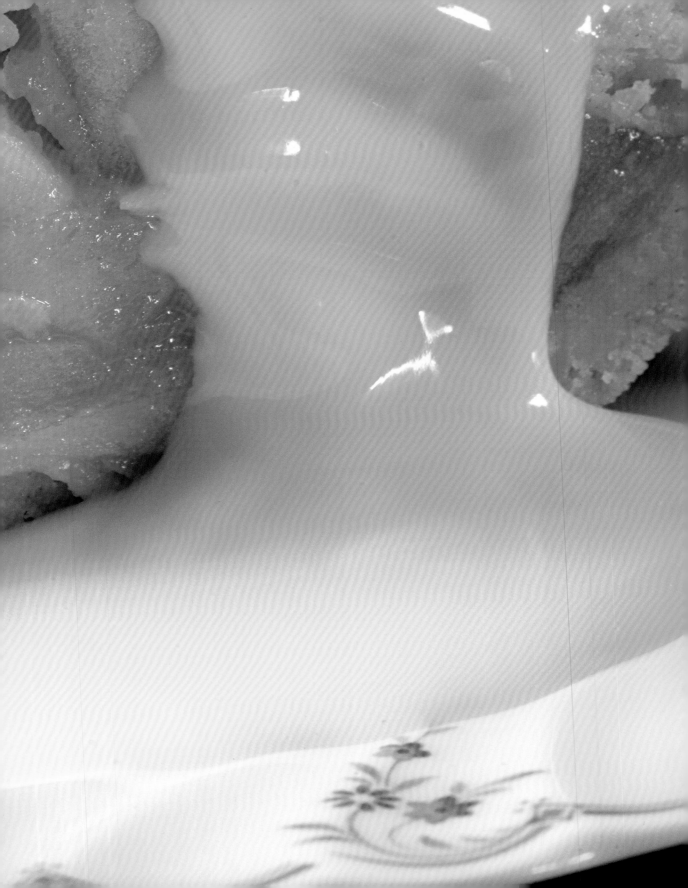

stirring custard

You can't beat home-made stirring custard served on top of a fruit-filled pie. It might not have that nostalgic bright yellow color but it tastes infinitely superior. I am sure there are some of you who will disagree and will seek out Bird's custard powder, or even ready-made custard instead, but for those who want to be converted, this is for you.

makes 2¹/2 cups/600ml

1 vanilla pod, split lengthwise, and the seeds scraped out with the point of a sharp knife and reserved · 2¹/2 cups/600ml whole milk · 4 egg yolks · 4 tbsp superfine sugar · 4 tsp cornstarch

Place the milk, vanilla pod, and its seeds in a heavy-bottomed saucepan and heat gently. Remove the pan from the heat and set aside for 20 minutes to allow the flavor of the vanilla to infuse the milk.

Place the egg yolks, sugar, and cornstarch in a bowl and beat together until smooth.

Remove the vanilla pod from the warm milk (wash it and keep it for reuse or store in a screwtop jar of superfine sugar to create vanilla sugar), then pour the milk onto the egg mixture, whisking as you go. Pour the mixture back into the saucepan and cook over a very low heat for about 8–10 minutes stirring constantly until the custard thickens and coats the back of the spoon, but don't allow it to boil.

If you are unlucky enough to curdle the custard, give the mixture a quick blast in a blender to bring it back together again.

Serve generously over your pie.

index

thankyou

There have been so many wonderful people who we have met and who have helped and inspired us along the long journey to this book and we would like to say a very heartwarming thankyou to you all—in particular the lovely Anna from Cassell Illustrated for believing in the project and letting us just get on with it! Sarah Dalkin, what can we say, you were with us all the way, and Helen Trent for letting us into her Aladdin's cave of props. And to all the wonderful people, producers and fanatics we have met and who have contributed and helped us along our pie journey: Andrew and Luke at Pokeno, Brighton—you make the best pies; Ian and Paul at Mrs King's, the only Melton Mowbray pork pie; William Rose our wonderful butcher in East Dulwich; Manzies on Tower Bridge Road, London—we will visit often; the mighty Grimsby Mariners, and Matty, for getting us through the barriers and into the world of soccer and pies; finally Typhoon for supplying us with the most gorgeous pie dishes (www.typhooneurope.com).

Angela's thankyous
I couldn't have made so many pies without the help and humor of the wonderful Jules—you were enthusiastic throughout, even when buried under pastry, thank you so much. Loving thanks to David Herbert for your invaluable advice, support, and enthusiasm and the fine collection of pie funnels. Jenny and Silvana, you are the best friends and support I could ever wish for. Big thanks to Mr James Fisher for all your help, advice and contacts. Biggest thanks ever has got to go to Vanessa for being there throughout and for sharing the pie vision.

So who did eat all the pies?
Dis and Alison for eating so many pies and loving every one, as well as returning the dishes clean; Col and Robert you were a joy to feed and such happy pie eaters; Jonathen and Penny for being troopers and managing to eat your way through a few with gusto; Gareth and Ruth whose enthusiasm for pie eating throughout was an inspiration.

Vanessa's thankyous
Thank you to Jamie, Luke and Rosie for their patience amongst so many pies and pictures. Craig, thank you for letting me get under your feet and so allowing me to get the shots. Most of all, I would like to thank Angela—who first came to me with the words 'Ness, I've got this idea, what do you think?', little did I realize what a wonderful road it would take us both down.